# The Digest Book of
# CANOEING

## By Charles J. Farmer

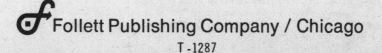Follett Publishing Company / Chicago

T-1287

## STAFF

*Editor*
  *Kathy Farmer*

*Production Manager*
  *Pamela J. Johnson*

*Associate Publisher*
  *Sheldon L. Factor*

## ACKNOWLEDGEMENTS

Kathy Farmer, wife, partner, editor and chief researcher is my constant source of encouragement and inspiration, and to her I owe the largest debt of gratitude.

I want to thank Deane Gray, of Old Town Canoe Company, for all his help, past and present.

To the experts, whose words of advice and experience are contained within, I wish the best of river running and sincere gratitude for taking the time to help me.

*Sincerely,*
*Charles J. Farmer*

ISBN 0-695-81287-4          **Library of Congress Card Number 79-50060**

# TABLE OF CONTENTS

# A History of Canoeing

### SKY, THE TREE RIDER

**HIS PEOPLE,** dwellers of the mountain caves, called him Sky, and his place and reputation were prominent. For it was Sky, at that time having accumulated 16 years on earth, who first rode the tree.

Broad chested, bow-legged Sky was watcher of the river—a job of considerable importance. He gauged rising waters, forewarning his people of imposing floods. During periods of low water, Sky discovered safe crossings to the other side of the river. There in late summer and early fall, his people could feast on the bounty of wild fruits and berries.

Sky was a river man. He knew the moods of the current. Not knowing how to swim according to our standards, he was an excellent floater and paddler,

imitating the movements of the trout, beaver and otter. Sky was a water creature, and he would ride the current like a nymph hatched from it. But his rides were short, not like that of the river otter, and this often depressed him. The water of the river, born fresh from the high peaks, was wonderfully clear and pure. But it was also so frigid that Sky's limbs would turn numb and blue, even on the warmest days.

Simple minds, attuned to living with nature did not, of course, pre-plan feats of great significance. It was just another day for Sky, who, for some instinctive reason, latched his muscular arms around the trunk of an uprooted floating tree. And he floated with the tree. His hands, arms and part of his shoulders were above the water surface, out of reach of the aching numbness of icy water. Sky shouted to no one in particular. He rode the log and felt the touch of current under his body.

The moon had burned its light. In darkness Sky discovered after many cold wet rides that by carefully mounting the log in shallow water, "gripping" the log with his inner thighs and paddling slowly with his feet, that he could ride the current for longer periods of time without rolling off the log. His rides became longer and longer. And by using his arms, he found he could change direction.

The dark phase passed, and the new moon came. It was time for Sky to show his people the riding tree. In his excitement, he rolled off the log with his first try and from the people came spontaneous moans and chattering. They drank the water from the river but had never floated in it like Sky. Some of them left. Again Sky mounted the log, this time more carefully. He floated toward the main current and then out of view. Some friends wept uncontrollably. Others ran along the banks and stayed with Sky and the floating log. He taught them to ride the log, and soon the tree and the river became tools.

Many, many moon phases passed before Filo, a man of high reasoning power, became disenchanted with the riding tree. He was often rolled off the log and drenched in the swift waters that typified his people's area. In the cold climate, where people wore loin cloths and capes of hide, the feet and legs of tree riders would ache with numbing pain. The very act of sitting on a round log was one that took skill, and it was nearly impossible to stand on most trees. Many baskets of fruit and roots had been lost in the river.

Filo selected three, beaver-felled logs of similar length. The logs, much smaller in diameter than the single tree boat, were old and partially rotted. Because thistle down and dried leaves floated high on the current, Filo reasoned that old, light logs would do the same. With strips of bark and simple knots, he lashed the logs together, front and back. Sitting on the log platform, he hand paddled into the mild current and was carried downstream. The precise balancing needed for the tree boat ride was a thing of the past. With feet propped on the two outside logs, he stood up and was amazed that the boat did not roll over.

With a long pole of poplar, Filo steadied the boat and guided it in any direction. The rest of the tribe copied Filo's discovery. Eventually custom accepted a new test for manhood—guide the lashed-log boat down the fastest water and ride the waves without losing balance.

The poplar pole was useless in deep water where the pole could not reach bottom. Then boats whirled in eddies and careened out of control, losing both men and craft. One day while observing the beaver, Filo became entranced by the broad, flat tail that propelled the beaver through the water. For two days he searched for a pole that flattened near the end. He further flattened the root end of the pole with a large rock, smashing the wood fibers into a shape much like the beaver's tail.

With the flattened pole, Filo sped through the rapids. Despite poor balance, crashing into a rock, and nearly upsetting his boat, Filo led the others through the raging torrent. Before long, all the boaters adopted the flattened poles. Filo won no more races. And the men soon found they could carry baskets of fruit and berries on their boats without fear of losing them to the angry river. The beaver logs became more efficient tools.

Fire had been sparked and men made warmth and cooked food for themselves. Inso, a strong youth of the valley people, was hunting for roots when he came upon a tree that had been charred by a great flash from the sky. After examining the blackened tree closely, he found it to be a great deal lighter than the logs used for tree boats or lashed-log boats. With a piece of bone, he easily scraped the charred wood from the felled tree. By the second day, Inso had carved a depression in the log, nearly deep enough for him to sit in. Inso gathered his family together to show them what he had done. Had the tree god taken away Inso's legs? They laughed when they realized Inso was sitting inside the tree. What a joke. Each took a turn sitting inside the silly tree seat.

A multitude of years passed before a descendant of Inso's tribe discovered the charred tree half buried in the sand. Like Filo, Tol was a reasonable man. People from many tribes sought Tol's advice. Despite its rough appearance, the carved-out tree intrigued Tol. He had long detested the often uncontrollable, slippery, wet lashed-log boats that were often at the mercy of the current. Besides the wind blowing them aimlessly about on the ponds and lakes, skins and kindling often became waterlogged when carried on unprotected lashed-log boats.

Tol recalled watching a chunk of cottonwood bark drift down the river. Used to scoop water from the river, cottonwood bark retains its rounded tree shape. The vision of the dugout came to life. Like the rounded sides of the bark, the dugout canoe would have enclosed and uplifted front and back, designed to slice through the water.

Finishing the job that Inso started, Tol and a helper lit small fires on the charred tree, further carving and hollowing out the trunk. With crude axes and scrapers, they shaped the dugout to a design and profile similar to today's canoes and kayaks. For the first time, men could sit or kneel inside a boat. They could be protected from current or wind-blown water. Their food and trading goods stayed dry. Flattened paddles, honed with stone and bone tools, would enable them to glide through the water.

Not too long ago, dugouts were equipped with outriggers for greater stability. Or two canoes were joined together by securing a platform between them. The double canoes, often equipped with sails, were the forerunners of the modern catamaran.

The giant cedar trees of the Pacific Northwest provided Indian tribes with the material to build dugouts, some of which were 60 feet long and were used for hunting whales.

Man progressed in boat building. Planks were placed edgewise and secured to the gunwales to make drier boats. The additional freeboard made larger loads possible.

In recent times in treeless regions canoes were constructed of wooden frames and covered with animal skins. The Plains Indians of North America built a circular canoe of buffalo hides. But the Eskimo kayak is the finest example of the covered frame canoe. Sealskin is stretched and sewn over a driftwood frame, leaving a small cockpit for the paddler. Kayaks are extremely seaworthy.

The skeletal frame of wood with a watertight cover of birch bark was perfected by the North American Indian. The birch canoe was light, fast, maneuverable and built in different sizes for various needs, from one-man boats to war canoes. Explorers using the birch bark design with minor modifications played a vital role in shaping the early history of the white man in North America. For about 200 years the canoe was the chief means of travel to remote and unexplored areas.

From birch bark the canoe progressed to the all-wood canoe in 1879, followed by the wood-frame, canvas-covered models. Plywood, pressed aluminum, fiberglass and plastic have taken over. The canoe is still very much with us. Thank you Sky, Filo, Inso and Tol.

Above—Pictographs along the Green River are a part of canoeing history. Below—If only the originators of the first canoes could see this.

# Is the Canoe for You?

**ASIDE FROM** all the basic realities of life, like family size, economics, portaging weight, available waters and special uses, I think most of us who choose the canoe as a lifelong friend have a bit of trapper blood in us.

Seldom do I dip the paddle into stream or lake, whether fishing, hunting or floating for the sake of floating, without dreaming a bit of the buckskin men who used the canoe and waterways for trapping and exploration. I am one of those men. Sometimes for scarcely a minute the spirit engulfs me. Other times, an entire day of canoe kinship passes before I realize the days of river trapping and pioneering are over. Or are they? Not as long as the canoe spirit lives. And live on I believe it will because this simple watercraft has gracefully endured the progressive stings of a sometimes venomous civilization. Motors just can't seem to drown out the slurp of a paddle slicing water. And the canoe, the boat of simple adventure, thrives in greater number now than it ever has. Break out the buckskins and glide.

## The Family Canoe

Ideally, canoeing is a two-person sport with paddlers in stern and bow for a well trimmed boat. The narrow beam of the craft, in comparison to other boats, is best suited to one person in the bow and one person in the stern in the sitting or kneeling paddling position.

Depending on the length of the canoe, with an average range of 12 to 20 feet, extra passengers are possible. A 17- to 20-foot long canoe can safely carry a family of four. However, to believe that any canoe has the stability of a rowboat or johnboat is foolish. A canoe with two passengers or four is safe only when the manufacturer's recommended weight capacity is followed and all passengers retain a low center of gravity. The kneeling paddling position is favored by skilled canoeists for this reason. Stability is increased, and paddling strokes can be used more effectively.

Where a kneeling or sitting position can be comfortable for paddling adults, the positions may not be favorites of the kids for any length of time. Canoe back rests and chairs, especially made to fit in the bottom of canoes for low center of gravity, can help relieve the fidgeting and cramped feeling that children get. The best technique, however, is teaching children why they must remain low and how their efforts can better balance the canoe. With short trips up to an hour in duration, there is usually not much of a problem. However, longer trips do pose problems that confront even the most patient parents and willing children. A canoe is just not the kind of craft where kids or adults can get up and stretch their legs. Periodic shore breaks help. But the best overall solution is to admit that, except for carrying small children, two canoes are better than one for the family of four or more. With good basic instruction, 10-year-olds and older can paddle their own canoes. Canoeing is meant to be a participation sport and few persons enjoy spectator roles.

### The Lone Canoeist

For the single man or woman, a canoe can be a good choice. Nothing can beat the feeling of a solitary float down a quiet, misty stream in early fall. Paddling from a position in the middle (amidship) of the canoe, the lone paddler can enjoy good boat control, even on relatively swift streams.

A good command of canoe strokes and sound understanding of stream navigation and water currents are necessary for the lone canoeist. If canoeing partners exhibit a good command of techniques, the single floater should be able to demonstrate them even better. Mild streams, ponds or lakes usually pose no threat to the lone paddler. However, common sense dictates that two paddlers are better than one in some situations, and there is safety and help in numbers. The most important decision the floater makes is correctly evaluating a certain stretch as safe and knowing that if

something does go wrong he or she can get out of the jam.

Another minor consideration for the solitary boater is the weight of the canoe for portaging and cartopping. With help not always readily available, choose a canoe you can handle.

### Canoe Advantages

A canoe has *shallow draft*. What that means simply is that it does not take much water to float a canoe. Where heavier, deeper boats with prominent, protruding keels hang up in shallow water, canoes with one or two paddlers on board can skim through. Canoes require water only a foot deep. Most canoes weigh under 90 pounds. Thus, the volume of water displaced (the weight of the displaced fluid being equal to that of the displacing body) is slight compared to heavier boats. As a result, the canoeing fisherman, hunter, camper, nature observer and photographer can glide over shallow back waters that would be impassable for conventional boats. Shallow draft also makes the canoe an ideal stream craft during low water periods in summer and fall. There will be times and places where dragging or portaging a canoe is necessary, but only when the riffles are barely trickling over the stream bed.

When compared to other boats, canoes are *light*. A 15-foot aluminum, Grumman Canoe of standard weight (they also come in lightweight models) weighs 69 pounds and is 35⅛ inches at the beam ( width of canoe at widest part). An Old Town Carleton fiberglass model of 16 feet weighs 79 pounds and has a beam of 36 inches. While an Old Town wood and canvas Guide model 18 feet long weighs 85 pounds and beams at 37 inches. Most adult men, acquainted with the techniques of lifting and leverage, can handle these weights without assistance when loading and unloading from cartop.

**FIBERGLASS**

Rail and Decks
Woven roving
Seat
Polyurethane Foam
Gelcoat
Fiberglass mat
Fiberglass mat
Keel
Fiberglass cloth
End grain balsa
Casco model shown. same as Oltonar.
Carleton Model decks, seats and gunwales

**OLTONAR**

Deck
Gunwale
Seat
Thwart
Rivet
Bolt
Vinyl Skin
ABS Substrates
Foam Core
ABS Substrates
Vinyl Skin
Foam expanded and formed to predetermined dimensions in carefully controlled heating and vacuum molding process
(See below)

**WOOD & FABRIC**

Stem Band
Gunwale (inside)
Deck
Seat
Thwart
Gunwale (outside)
Rail
Rib
Canvas or reinforced plastics
Keel
Planking

VINYL SKIN
SUBSTRATE
SUBSTRATE
CORE MATERIAL
SUBSTRATE
SUBSTRATE
VINYL SKIN

COMPONENT LAYERS — LAMINATED INTO SHEETS — HEATED AND FORMED

DIAGRAM of "Old Town Canoe"

STEM BAND
INSIDE STEM
BOW DECK 16 INCH
BOW SEAT CANED
BOW THWART
SECTION OF FLOOR RACK
OPEN GUNWALE CONSTRUCTION
RIBS
PLANKING
OUTER GUNWALE
STERN THWART
SECTION OF HALF RIBS
INNER GUNWALE
STERN SEAT CANED
INSIDE STEM
STEM BAND
STERN DECK 16 INCH

Diagram of a canoe and the different types of construction and materials available.

The sport canoe by Grumman takes motors and is a stable compromise between canoe and rowboat.

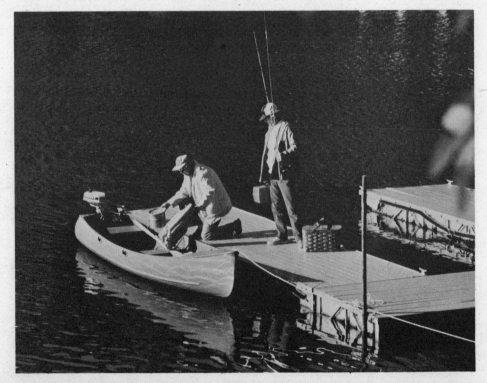

Average 3-foot beams make storage, even in limited apartment dwellings, possible. Two canoes can be carried on a standard size vehicle and compacts can easily handle one canoe. Portaging, with the aid of a homemade or commercially manufactured carrying yoke, can be handled by a man of average strength with little difficulty for distances up to a mile. And some canoeists swear it is easier to portage a canoe by themselves, on their own back, than sharing the load with a partner. Either way, canoes are light enough to be easily handled by one or two people, without the aid of a special trailer, hoist or winch.

Modern canoes, made of aluminum, fiberglass or plastic, require *little or no upkeep*. Interior and exterior finishes can be protected and kept nice looking with occasional applications of paste wax. Canoes should be stored under some kind of shelter on racks or boards that keep them from contact with the ground. Wood and canvas canoes, still manufactured commercially by the Old Town Canoe Company, Old Town, Maine, require more upkeep. They must be protected by varnish or paint. The beauty, tradition and workmanship inherent in the wood-canvas canoe often instills a strong sense of maintenance pride in its owners. Upkeep then, for some, is a matter of personal satisfaction and the true worth of the canoe increases with age and use.

Excellent quality canoes, from 12 to 20 feet in length, fall into a general price range extending from $200 (for a

Above—The canoe makes an excellent lake craft— easy to paddle. Right—Family size may dictate that two canoes are needed. Below—The lone paddler uses small 12-footer to fish from and portage.

Above—Sailing rigs can be purchased as canoe option. Right—Some canoes have Styrofoam flotation strips on the exterior. Below—This 15-footer is fine for two persons. It's made of polyethylene.

used model) to $500 for 18- or 20-footers. Good paddles of ash, spruce or maple cost $10 to $30. More expensive paddles are required for white water. Coast Guard approved personal flotation devices (P.F.D.s) for each canoeist and bow and stern ropes round out the basic gear. Good cartop carriers can be purchased for under $30. Nothing is really cheap these days, but it is reassuring for prospective canoeists to know that most modern canoes are high quality products. A canoe can last a lifetime. Considering the enjoyment and adventure a canoe can give, the initial investment (most often under $400) seems small in comparison. Add to these facts. the beauty of swift, gas-less, paddle propulsion, and we

have a craft that is cheap to run and maintain. The canoeist does have a gas or electric motor option. Canoeing can be truly simple and uncluttered and that's the joy of it.

Because the canoe is silent, because it does not need fuel for propulsion, and because it seems to fit into the natural scheme of things outdoors, it is *the* ideal sport of streams and lakes. For the peaceful fisherman who gauges his success on a quality experience, for the stalking hunter steeped in the tradition of trapper times, for the camper who craves solitude and river spirit, and for the nature observer and photographer who likes natural contact still and up close, the canoe is for you.

# How to Choose the Right Canoe

EVALUATED on their own merits, there are few, if any, "bad" canoes—most name brand craft are quality products. However canoes can be classified according to stability, construction, safety features, and maneuverability. They can also be judged on how well they perform certain functions. For instance, one brand or model might be better for lake or pond use rather than for white water.

As a novice canoeist in the initial stages of canoe buying, all boats might look basically the same. But closer investigation begins to turn up differences. And as small as those differences might be, they can be important. After some simple, basic research, the prospective canoeist soon discovers that the type of keel on a particular model, for example, better suits the boat for lakes rather than for rivers.

Canoes, though basically simple in design, often have subtle features that account for the hows and whys of boat performance. As a prospective buyer, the secret to sound buying is to look closely. Avoid fancy frills, and expect sound, definite answers to all your questions. Reading several canoe manufacturers' catalogs in advance of actual shopping can help. Here's a general guideline.

## Brands

Canoes reach brand name status by producing good quality products for a number of years. Some companies have a multitude of years under their thwarts; others, because of demand, innovation and good advertising have earned fine reputations in relatively few years. However, do not choose your canoe solely on the reputation of the boat builder, rather purchase a canoe that meets *your* personal needs. Some name brands you will come across are Old Town, Grumman, Lund, Sawyer, Mad River, Lowe Line, Alumacraft, Sea Nymph, Michi-Craft and Smoker-Craft. Some companies specialize in certain materials for building

Aluminum canoes are durable and require little upkeep.

Above—Some aluminum canoes can be ordered painted in a variety of colors. Right—White water canoes have shallow keels and extra ribs. Below—Small, 10- and 12-footers are fine for portaging and pond use.

Above—Folding kayaks for two or one solve transportation and storage problems. Left—Some canoes and kayaks can be easily converted to sailing rigs. Below—Square end canoe has transom designed to easily mount an outboard motor.

New synthetic plastic canoes are durable and light.

their products like aluminum, fiberglass, plastic or wood and canvas. New multi-laminates, like Kevlar and Oltonar are becoming increasingly popular for canoe hulls. Your choice of canoe depends somewhat on the type of material used for its construction.

### Hull Materials

**Aluminum** canoes are rugged. They will stand up to a good deal of abuse and require relatively little or no upkeep. They are subject to denting and, under moderate to heavy white water use, when pinned in the current by rocks or logs, can bend in two beyond repair. Some "thin-skinned" lightweight canoes, not really recommended for heavy white water use, are also susceptible to puncturing by rocks. Certain aluminum hulls have rough edges which could prove dangerous in a hasty exit. Aesthetically speaking, the unpainted silver hull has not been awarded any beauty prizes. They also have been described as "loud" because sound is easily carried through aluminum. Several manufacturers offer color options at prices ranging from $30 to $50 extra. The average weight of a 17-foot double-end aluminum canoe is 75 pounds.

**Fiberglass** canoes are durable and require little or no upkeep. They are more susceptible to river running abrasions and cracking than quality aluminum boats are. Contrary to popular belief, fiberglass boats are not generally lighter than aluminum ones. On the contrary, depending on the model, length and construction, the average fiberglass craft weighs a few pounds more than an aluminum one of comparable size. Fiberglass canoes are "softer" and "quieter" than the rather harsh aluminum ones. They do not conduct cold or heat as aluminum canoes do nor do they have the rough appearance and edges of aluminum. Built from molds, they do not have rivets and therefore appear more "finished" than aluminum. Colors are softer and richer in appearance due to impregnation of pigments into fiberglass resin. The average weight of a 17-foot double-end fiberglass canoe is 80 to 85 pounds.

The Old Town Canoe Company still makes high quality **wood and canvas** canoes. As Old Town puts it, "Wood and canvas is for those special people who believe in tradition and appreciate the beauty of wooden craft and the skill that goes into their construction." Enough said. The sight of a wood n' canvas makes me drool. However, they are more than double the price of good aluminum or fiberglass craft. Lighter than fiberglass, they are ideal for lakes and slow streams and aesthetically cannot be touched by any other canoe, but they are susceptible to rips, cracking and warping when not properly cared for. They are a dream to paddle—soft and quiet. Old Town makes five different wood and canvas models. An 18-foot "Guide" model by Old Town weighs 85 pounds and is a graceful creature.

**The Synthetics**—ABS plastic, polyethylene, Kevlar, and Oltonar—are new canoe materials. They are super tough substances that excel in many ways. They are virtually indestructible, unsinkable and, when trapped in currents of heavy force, they do not fold or crack. Extremely heavy blows may cause dents, but these can be removed with application of heat. There is no up-keep or maintenance, save an occasional washing for the sake of cosmetics.

My 17-foot 2-inch Chipewyan Oltonar canoe, by Old Town, has undergone punishment of all kinds with little evidence of wear and no punctures or leaks to date. The tough, synthetic shell weighs 77 pounds and has out-dueled rocks, logs, gravel and collisions of all descriptions. In the event of deep gouges and punctures, Old Town sells Oltonar repair kits, which through quick, minor sealing, sanding and drying render the rugged crafts good as new.

### Length Dependent on Use

There are short canoes (10-14 feet.), mid-length (15-17 feet), and long canoes (18-20 feet). Short canoes weighing 30 to 50 pounds are fine for kids or for solo paddling. They are easy to launch, paddle, portage, and are good for one-man fishing floats. For camping, their load-carrying capacity is limited.

The mid-length canoes are good all-around canoes for general family use, lake or pond fishing, and stream running. Ideal for two people, there is moderate load space to handle fishing gear and camping equipment. These canoes weigh from 55 to 80 pounds.

The long canoes may weigh 85 to 120 pounds, on the heavy side for an inexperienced portager. However they make excellent expedition canoes for extended camping and fishing trips. Ample cargo space provides room for the necessities as well as a few luxuries. Generally speaking, the longer the canoe, the faster and the better it tracks. The long canoes are good for big lake travel and for running wide, swift rivers. Use in tight white water, filled with rock gardens and logs, is limited because of slow maneuverability and length.

However, the longer canoes cannot necessarily hold more passengers. More cargo, that can be carefully stowed for good trim, yes. Two people per boat is ideal. For family use, consider two mid-length canoes rather than one long boat. The mid-length canoes and especially the 17-footers are certainly the best all-around choices.

### Choice of Keels

A keel, the reinforcing ridge down the center of most canoes, comes basically in two different styles. A standard keel enhances the forward tracking stability of a canoe, particularly in crosswinds. If most of your canoe travel will be on lakes or on long, deep river trips, the standard keel is for you.

There are also flat, shoe (or shallow draft) keels that give some tracking stability yet do not significantly affect side-to-side maneuverability. (Side-to-side maneuvering is seriously hampered by standard keels which offer lateral resistance to the water.) The shallow draft keel, or no keel at all, is for paddling in moving water or white water running. It is less likely to catch on shoal obstructions and provides more protection to the bottom of a canoe than a narrow, deep keel. The flat shoe or shallow draft keel is about ⅜-inch deep.

### Folding Canoes or Boats

Boats with wooden frames and special canvas or hypalon skins that fold or pack for storage, comprise a special category of canoes. They display similar characteristics to rigid hull canoes.

### Things to Do Before Canoe Purchase

1. Rent as many different types of canoes (constructed of various materials) as possible.
2. Collect brochures of leading canoe manufacturers and compare statistics and features.
3. Determine what your intended use is and select a craft that fits your needs.
4. Make sure rivets are well secured, of good design and properly spaced on aluminum canoes.
5. Ragged edges and sharp metal on aluminum canoes are signs of inferior workmanship.
6. Compare canoe warranties. Lifetime warranties, under normal use, are standard.
7. Good used canoes sell for about half the price of new ones. Beware of popped rivets or aluminum patching. A few dents won't hurt.

# Canoe Equipment

**CANOEING IS** simple sport in its purest form. Besides the boat itself, paddles and Coast Guard approved flotation devices are the only equipment necessary.

Canoeists themselves, though, differ extensively in tastes and desires, needs and skills. As a result, canoe equipment manufacturers produce a broad variety of items that can add comfort, convenience, safety and enjoyment to the sport. In evaluating equipment, consider your own needs. What may be considered a gimmick by some, may be a necessity to others.

### Paddles

A variety of paddles are available to canoeists. Construction and material determine whether a paddle can be rated poor, fair, or good. Single blade paddles are most commonly used, while double blades are fine for solo cruising against rather consistent strong winds and waves. Top grade wooden paddles are made of selected pieces of spruce, ash or maple. Sections are glued to-

Below—T-handle fiberglass paddle and wooden canoe paddles. Right—Synthetic paddles.

gether with the grain of the wood kept flat in the blade. The wood grain in the shaft is placed at right angles to the blade. This arrangement strengthens the paddle and increases its durability.

Inexpensive paddles, often advertised as "bargain" items, are usually mass-produced from a single piece of wood and are heavier than composite wood paddles. Some are made of spruce, but, more commonly, soft woods like pine, cedar and fir are used. Hardwood paddles can withstand much contact abuse in shallow water, whereas softwood will chip, splinter and crack. Quality hardwood paddles are your best buy. A good spare paddle should always be carried.

Wooden paddles sometimes are fiberglass or aluminum tipped for extra protection against bottom contact. Also, the shaft of the paddle can be fitted with a leather or fiberglass chafing collar near the throat.

Besides wood, paddles can be made of fiberglass, aluminum, ABS plastic and Kevlar, and various combinations of these materials. Such paddles are better choices than inferior wood paddles for most canoeing needs. They require no upkeep and have strength and durability. Paddles with some built-in flex, whether wood or synthetic, are favored over stiff paddles. The only way to discover various degrees of flex in paddles is to try out as many different brands as possible. The flex quality will not be as obvious to a novice canoeist as it will be to an experienced paddler, but it is important for good feel and satisfying rhythm on extended cruises or lake paddling.

### Personal Paddle Fit

*Rules of thumb:* The distance from the paddler's nose to the ground measures the approximate length of a proper paddle fit. Or, the length of the paddle should span the outstretched arms with the fingers curled over the tip of the blade and the end of the grip. Give or take an inch or two, these two rules produce similar results.

### Cartop Carriers

For the transportation of one or two canoes, the cartop carrier is standard equipment. Canoes are light

Above left—Most standard size passenger vehicles can easily handle two canoes. Above right—Cartop carrier of aluminum with attachments for carrying canoes on edge. Right—Foam block type carrier clamps on boat's gunwales, holds firm.

enough and have a narrow enough beam to be transported easily on the roof of a vehicle—a trailer is unnecessary. It is important to select a cartop carrier that fits the car securely. An ill-fitting carrier, poor tie-downs, and faulty lashing techniques can cause dangerous shifting of the load and possible loss of the craft.

Basically there are about three different types of carriers. For vehicles without rain gutters, rubber pads or suction cups grip the roof while vinyl-covered clamps fasten to the door frame. Another type clamps or screws down into the rain gutter. A new model, by Grumman, called the CanoeTopper, consists of four sponge vinyl blocks that snap onto the boat's gunwales. With two lines and four side hooks the canoe is tightly secured to the car's roof with a minimum of wind resistance.

Carriers have extruded aluminum or wooden crossbars on which the canoe rests. Old Town Canoe Company has a contoured boat rack available as an option that fits on their carrier.

A few things to remember about cartopping: Always try to obtain help in putting the canoe on and taking it off the rack. Boats are always topped upside down or bottom up. And tie-down lines from each end of the canoe should be tightly secured to the car. In addition to the rack itself being clamped to the car, vertical tie-downs attached to one side of the rack, stretched over the canoe and secured on the other side of the rack complete cartop rigging. Commercially made tie-downs hold boats securely fore and aft and eliminate time wasted in tying and untying knots. Shock cords, because of stretch, do not qualify for fore and aft tie-down material. Quarter-inch cotton or Dacron line does the job best. It's a good idea, on long trips, to check carrier clamping systems and tie-down ropes periodically.

## Trailers

A variety of flatbed or stacked rail trailers are used to transport one or more canoes. Persons with bad backs, those canoeing alone, or where help is usually not available for cartop loading and unloading often choose simple, two-wheel trailers. A trailer is especially nice if it can also be used for purposes besides canoe transportation. Trailers made especially for hauling several canoes or racks custom-built of steel can be purchased commercially. They are especially suited for scouting groups, canoe outfitters, and expeditions. As with cartopping, canoes must be secured tightly in racks for safety and to prevent damage. For short hauls, some

Conventional boat trailer can be used to haul canoes.

Specialized trailers can carry group canoes.

pickup truck beds adequately handle one or two canoes. Too often, though, the canoe extends over the tailgate, thus requiring special care to cushion and tightly lash the boat down to tarp hooks and bumper.

### Motor Brackets

Outboard motor brackets for gasoline or electric powered engines are made of metal and wood and clamp to the gunwales of most double-end canoes without any structural changes. Most canoe manufacturers have their own brackets that are especially designed and fitted to their boats. The addition of a motor may be handy for covering large stretches of lake or flat river water and for fishing.

Aluminum canoe equipped with lateen sail, rudder, mast and leeboards.

### Sailing Rigs

Most canoes can be converted to sailing rigs with a minimum of structural changes. The addition of a sailing rig can add a new and exciting dimension to your canoe. The Grumman Canoe Company offers a convenient sailing package that fits their factory prepared canoes. Either 45-square foot lateen or 65-square foot gunter rigs can be used. Aluminum mast, boom, sail, leeboards, spreader bar, rudder, and adapter and rigging lines come in the package. A screwdriver and pliers are the only tools required for converting the canoe into a sailboat.

### Rowing Attachments

Some manufacturers offer optional rowing attachments that clamp to the gunwales. Other rowing attachments can be custom-made. Rowing rigs are not meant to replace paddling as much as to add speed and power to long flat lake trips and for solo fishing from a canoe. Oars about 7 feet long are used with most canoe rowing rigs.

### Carrying or Portaging Yokes

Carrying yokes of wood or metal with cushioned pads that rest on the shoulders can make the difference between miserable and fairly comfortable portaging. Although life preservers, rolled up jackets and shirts can make the job easier, the yokes are far more stable and comfortable. Available from some manufacturers or home-made, they can be mounted on center thwarts. Wooden crossbar yokes are far more comfortable than metal.

### Kneeling Pads

Without a cushioned pad, kneeling is uncomfortable in a canoe. Pads should provide some type of ventilation at the point of contact. Kneel pads or protectors sold in sporting goods stores are adequate for short runs. Large cellulose sponges are good and so is raw foam rubber, at least 4 inches thick or doubled for added cushion.

### Seats or Backrests

Metal, or even better, wooden seats and backrests are sold by manufacturers and make sitting much more comfortable for passengers. Floors of aluminum canoes especially can become very cold and sometimes wet. Besides being built for comfort, good seats encourage a low center of gravity.

### Cargo Bags

Waterproof, watertight bags of heavy-duty plastic keep gear safe and dry. Some feature canvas or nylon interior or exterior linings. Look for sturdy construction, carrying handle, and strong lash loops.

Canoe seats, seat back, carrying yoke and outboard motor mount.

### Portage Packs

Nylon rucksacks or cargo bags with sturdy backpack straps (padded for loads over 10 pounds) can keep hands free when portaging. Food, extra clothing, first aid kit, camera, and fishing tackle can be packed in portage packs.

### Canoe Caddies

Rather large, lightweight rubber tires and frame with bicycle-type spoked wheels strap or clamp to the canoe for portaging or transporting over short distances. Handy in permanent or semi-permanent camp or landing areas where solo portaging is the rule rather than the exception.

### Add-on Pontoons

Foam pads clamp on to the gunwales for additional stability and flotation in rough water or when carrying heavy loads. Not a bad precaution when carrying small children as passengers. Some canoes are manufactured with foam strips attached to the hull. They are not to be confused with the accessory pads.

### Anchors

Any anchor up to 5 pounds of either a folding or mushroom type holds a canoe in calm water or slow currents for fishing or photography purposes. Vinyl covered anchors are quiet and eliminate rough edges.

### Poles

Wooden, fiberglass or aluminum poles, 12 feet long, propel a canoe in shallow water either upstream or downstream. Until recently, poling was somewhat of a lost art.

Left—Expedition cargo pack. Below—A canoe camping pack. Both are waterproof.

# Canoe Strokes

AS WITH most sports requiring knowledge and skill, there is a right and a wrong way of paddling. Novices, first introduced to canoeing, ordinarily do what comes naturally. Whether in the bow or stern position, they jab the paddle into the water, close to the canoe and pull the blade towards their position in the boat. Not bad, really, for this simple stroke will propel them in adequate fashion. If bow and stern paddlers are fairly synchronized—which is possible after a bit of practice—strokes can be smooth and some fair distances can be covered. Hopefully, this practice session is conducted in a pool, pond or lake. The absence of even mild currents enables the canoeists to track in a relatively straight line to a given destination or turn on a desired course. For some novices that's the extent of paddling skills, especially if they are limited to lakes. Beginners feel the ''jab and pull'' to be all that is needed to propel a canoe.

When introduced to stream cruising, it becomes dramatically obvious that there is more to canoe paddling than meets the eye. The addition of a current, however mild, makes instruction necessary. It's like the skier who without instruction has the strength and agility to ''work'' a small hill. But, presented with a significant grade, a long run, and a few trees to negotiate, the novice using muscle alone usually meets with disaster. It is not until the skier learns the moves, edges, angles, and harnesses the down grade to skill and knowledge that the mountain can be mastered. The same with canoeing. Stroking is more than pure muscle. It is harnessing the current to the paddle—getting the angle, the edge, the course of most or least water resistance.

There is a distinct type of stroke for nearly every type of current situation and to enjoy the full thrill of canoeing, and save a lot of needless ''pure muscle'' work, learning the full complement of strokes is worth the effort. It is reassuring for women and children, who may lack the pure physical strength, to realize that the

The foundation to good stroking is the kneeling position and a good, low center of gravity.

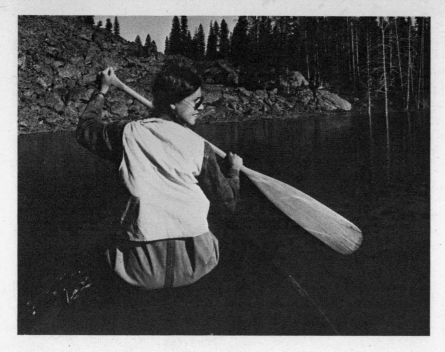

Here is proper grip on paddle displayed by author's wife.

knowledge of stroking and the currents can put them on nearly equal stream-running terms with men.

Strokes can be learned from books and from the guidelines that follow here. But, the fastest, most practical way to learn them is from qualified instructors in a canoe safety program. The American National Red Cross, through their Small Craft Safety program, is one such organization that offers basic instruction. Men, women and children can participate. Families can enroll in the same course for added enjoyment and a solid canoeing education for the future.

### 10 Basic Canoe Strokes

Depending on terminology, there are basically 10 canoe strokes that should be learned and practiced until they become nearly reflex actions. Precisely, when and where to use the various strokes takes on-stream practice—because rivers and currents are different, strokes will also vary. Canoeists soon find that various strokes can be modified to fit particular water and weather conditions.

*Forward* and *backward* strokes, executed in the same way but in opposite directions, are counted simply as one stroke. The *J-Stroke, Steering* or *Rudder, Draw, Cross-draw, Cross-backstroke, Scull, Pry, Sweep* and *Inverted Sweep* are the techniques to learn.

Strokes are made with one hand cupped on the grip of the paddle and the other on the shaft several inches above the blade. A general rule to follow for the distance between grips is the distance from the paddler's armpit to the tips of the fingers. When the distance is right, a paddler can usually *feel* good power and some paddle flex when strokes are made. It is a good idea to practice strokes both right- and left-handed as this will

increase proficiency and stamina. When not making strokes, hold the paddle horizontally across the gunwales in the "ready" position or keep it in the water as a keel for stability in rough stretches.

Possibly one of the best habits you can develop is learning the basic strokes from a kneeling position (use cushions or knee pads while learning). Not only will your center of gravity be lower, affording more stability, but the kneeling position is highly recommended for running any kind of white water. Since modern canoes have to be ordered special *without* seats, most of us, when learning paddling strokes, assumed that everything done in a canoe is from the sitting position. More power can be put into strokes from the kneeling position because of more efficient and easier torso movements. In the kneeling position, rest your buttocks against the thwart or the edge of the seat. This low kneeling position is a good brace for extra stability and for absorbing impact with obstacles in the river. Strokes should be practiced and learned first in lakes, ponds, or flat stream water.

### 1. FORWARD AND BACKWARD STROKES

Forward and backward paddling strokes should be made parallel to the gunwale with a solid bite or catch of the flat blade with a smooth continuous stroke. At the end of the stroke, the bottom hand will be about even with the hip with all the power having been applied at that point. Both arms are then relaxed and the blade is withdrawn from the water at a "feathered" angle to the water for a smooth, nearly dragless recovery, and the stroke is repeated. Backstrokes for backward maneuvering alone or for stopping or moving backward with a partner, is done in the same way, with the blade feathered out upon the forward recovery.

## 2. J-STROKE

The final part of the basic pull stroke, an outward curve or "J" counteracts the push of the forward stroke, enabling a lone canoeist to hold a straight course. The more vertical the stroke (that is, not angled but using the hips and back for placement), the more effective it will be for keeping course. Some canoeists execute this stroke so well, an observer would swear there's an invisible bow paddler helping to keep the boat on track.

## 3. STEERING OR RUDDER STROKE

This is the stroke that looks and feels good, especially for a novice sternsman in swift water. It's easy to make because the blade of the paddle is held firmly in the water at the stern for a rudder. However, the steer-ing stroke should be used for only minor course changes since it slows headway considerably (sometimes desirable) and is best applied when approaching landings. A bow rudder can also be used to move the bow sharply toward the paddle side when the paddle is angled about 20 degrees from the bow. There will be a lot of water pressure on the bow blade in this stroke so it is advisable to brace the paddle shaft on the gunwale.

## 4. DRAW STROKE

The draw stroke accomplishes movement to the side the paddle is working on. Start the stroke as far out from the gunwale as you can reach, with the blade facing the gunwale, and draw the paddle towards you. In this stroke, you are actually pulling the canoe to the paddle. In swift current, where sideways maneuverability is

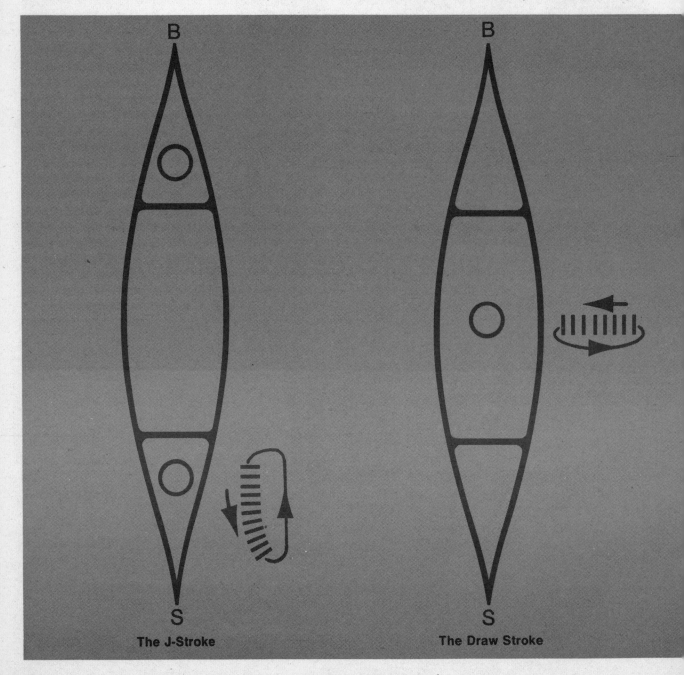

The J-Stroke                    The Draw Stroke

vital, the draw is the most important and powerful stroke in canoeing. It can be modified to a variety of angles. Bow and stern paddlers draw together on the same side to maneuver the canoe directly sideways or on opposite sides to execute a pivot turn.

## 5. CROSS-DRAW

This stroke is performed more efficiently at the bow than stern or amidship. The paddler pivots at the waist and swings the paddle over the canoe to make a draw stroke on the opposite side of the canoe without shifting his grip. This stroke enables you to pull your end of the canoe to either side.

## 6. CROSS-BACKSTROKE

This stroke permits back paddling on either side without changing the grip. It is similar to the cross-draw but differs because the stroke draws from the stern toward the bow.

## 7. SCULL

An alternative to the draw strokes, sculling is used for movement to the side. As in a draw, the paddle is away from the hull. The blade is then worked in a forward-backward manner, alternating blade angle as the paddle is pulled steadily toward the boat. The blade action puts pressure on the blade face nearest the canoe and draws the canoe toward the paddle. The action is reversed to move the canoe away from the paddling side. In sculling, a paddler leans somewhat on the paddle for effective stroking.

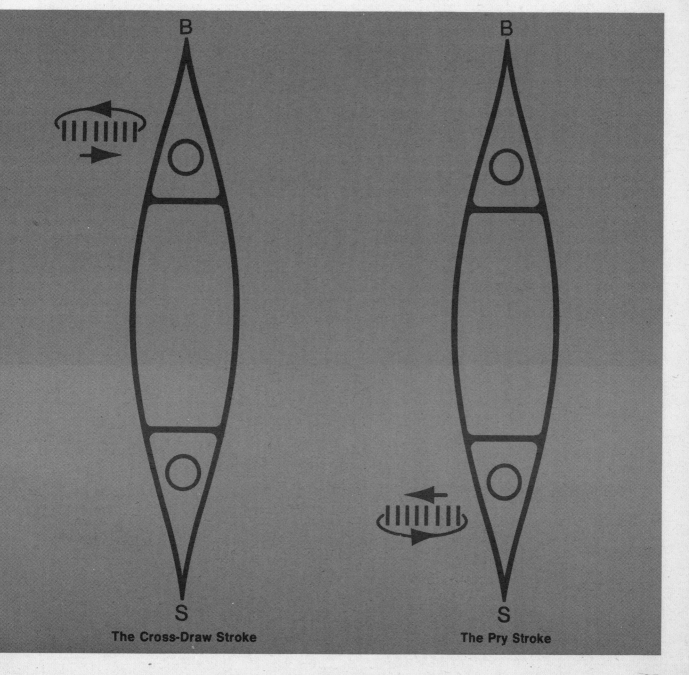

The Cross-Draw Stroke                    The Pry Stroke

## 8. PRY

This is an effective stern stroke for side movement or turning because the blade has powerful leverage. A strong outward motion is necessary for making this stroke effective. It is a good stability stroke since a paddler need not change sides in heavy water. It is, however, not as powerful as the draw stroke. Because of the angle of the paddle and stroke, it can capsize a canoe if paddle and rock or limb make contact in shallow water.

## 9. SWEEP

This is a wide arc stroke used for power and turning. Single paddlers, near amidship use the sweep of a 180-degree arc, well out from gunwale to a finish near the boat, for sharp canoe turns. A stern sweep traces the forward path of an arc, beginning close to the gunwale and ending away from it to complete the arc. A back sweep, in bow or stern, is the reverse of the forward sweep.

## 10. INVERTED SWEEP

The stroke begins like a bow draw, then blossoms into a sharply hooked J-stroke while sweeping next to the gunwale at midpoint in its arc. This is a good stroke to use for turning sharply toward the paddle side when paddling from the center of the canoe.

At first, strokes should be thought-out techniques to match the type of water. But it does not take long for them to become second nature.

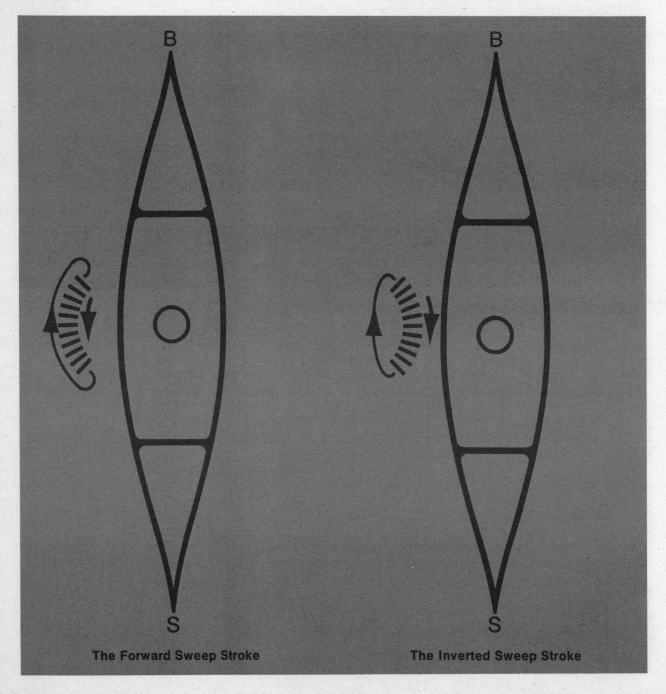

The Forward Sweep Stroke                    The Inverted Sweep Stroke

Left—The real enjoyment of canoeing comes with knowledge of proper strokes. Note follow-through on sweep. Above— Here's the start of the forward sweep stroke. Below—Bow paddler starts draw stroke and stern paddler changes sides. The dog is dog-paddling, obviously.

# Poling—A Tradition

CANOE POLING is a tradition that is not widely known or used even among canoeists. The American Canoe Association sponsors national poling competition, and good polers are a pleasure to watch. The most satisfying poling, though, comes from doing rather than observing. It is a technique that can be self-taught if a few rules of the pole are followed. A comprehensive book on the subject, *Canoe Poling* by Al, Syl & Frank Beletz, is a good guide to follow. The book can be ordered for $4.95 from the Mackenzie River Company, Box 9301, Richmond Heights Station, St. Louis, MO. 63117.

The setting pole is a low water tool used to navigate shallow rocky streams, ponds or lakes where a paddle can't really get a good bite on the water. Al Beletz, American Canoe Association Poling Chairman estimates most small streams generally have an average poling depth of 4 to 12 inches. "Ideal for probing from the standing position."

Standing in a canoe? Yes. The pole is used to snub, check and alter downstream travel. For upstream maneuvering, the pole bites against the bottom to drive the canoe forward against the water.

Any shallow stream, under 4 feet deep, makes an ideal poling course. Polers can navigate upstream or downstream in 4 inches of water or more, where paddles are awkward and impractical. Few streams are uniformly shallow or deep. Most waterways have deep sides and shallow sides. Sometimes the shallows are in the middle of a river. Either way, the poler searches for, and usually finds, just the right depth for poling and grabbing the bottom. Combining poling and paddling, for thorough enjoyment of various stretches of the same river, makes for a complete canoeist.

Poling can be used to navigate streams considered too narrow or too shallow for standard paddling techniques. A simple pole, 10-14 feet in length made of straight grained spruce or aluminum, opens up a new and different world of stream running.

Small stream navigation can be a pleasurable, slow-paced, intimate relationship with the often secretive world of meandering water courses. A poler gets close to stream life in and along the water. There is time to get involved. Birds, animals, and fish take on a special meaning, and the poler becomes *part* of the environment rather than an observer. It is a floating world in miniature. But best of all, both downstream and upstream, poling is possible.

It is the constant snubbing action of the pole on a downhill run that keeps the canoe on course. This is a skill acquired mostly by feel. An open canoe, 15 to 17 feet in length, is fine for poling. Regardless of the size, the downstream end of the canoe should be trimmed so it will stay in alignment with the current. A single poler can stand behind the center thwart when going upstream and just in front of the center thwart when running downstream. Without trimming, either by body positioning or cargo, canoes will turn broadside.

Whether going upstream or downstream, the pole is pushed, used as a paddle (the kayak stroke) or snubbed, to keep the canoe in a controlled course. The pole can also be used to brake the canoe to a complete stop while going upstream. On slow downstream runs, medium pressure can be put on the pole for sure stops. Swifter runs require a series of braking snubs, similar in many ways to pumping the brakes of a car.

Sylvester Beletz, past National Poling Champion, utilizing his collapsible aluminum pole and specially designed poling canoe in Meramec River rapids. Photo by Al Beletz

Sitting—
Kayak Stroke

Standing—
Windmill Stroke

Kneeling—
Kneeling Stroke

Frank Beletz, utilizing his collapsible aluminum pole heads upstream. Exploring the small streams and upper stretches, too shallow for paddling, is the safest way to canoe, both summer and winter.

### Standing or Sitting

Poling seems to violate the commandment, "never stand up in a canoe." The pole however, is not only used as a snubber and pusher, but also as crutch and balancing stick. According to expert poler, Al Beletz, whose company manufactures the famous 12-foot collapsible aluminum Sylvester pole, "A standing poler has his whole body and legs to counterbalance, while a paddler has only the upper body to work with. Once the initial fear of standing and rocking back and forth in a canoe is overcome (with practice), standing and good balance become second nature. Downstream visibility is excellent." Foot and body balance is especially important. The foot on the poling side should be slightly forward of the other foot—and with the feet at least 12 inches apart for good balance. A pair of deck shoes or boating moccasins with nonskid soles aids surefootedness. Barefoot poling can be slippery.

Standing is the traditional method of poling and the trickiest to master. However, a poler in the standing position has good pole angle for quick, strong snubbing downstream and upstream pushing. Standing in a canoe requires good balance, quite similar to downhill skiing in that flex at the knees (to absorb the jolts) and a looseness at the hips with responsive weight shifting right and left, are the ingredients for good balance.

The standing poler has the advantage of being able to better see the course downstream or upstream. When poling from a standing position, a canoeist feels like he is walking on water. The entire body and all the senses are alert to the boat and the current underfoot.

Sitting kayak-type of strokes can also be used when poling downstream, using a lightweight aluminum pole. Upstream pushing from the sitting position can be used in slow currents. Moderate to swift currents, however, require standing or kneeling, again with the boat trimmed downstream. Finding the course of least resistance is a constant and entertaining challenge in upstream poling. The middle of the river most commonly displays the strongest current, so the poler seeks the edge of the current and side eddies closest to shore.

A rather wide grip is required to insure good arm and shoulder movement, which in turn assures solid *downstream* snubbing *jabs* and efficient *upstream pushing* strokes. Choose the grip and leverage that feels best to you. But remember not to use the pole in front of your body, but rather to the side when shoulders and hips are rotated. The snubbing end of the pole if hooked or caught only momentarily on the bottom could be enough to throw you off balance and into the water. Work the pole to one side or the other and don't get caught behind it.

One does not have to be a purist poler to enjoy this delightful change of pace. In fact, the combination of pole and paddle serves nicely on many small and medium float streams. And the combination of the two techniques adds immensely to the pleasure of the total canoeing experience. Used as a fishing tool, the poler-fisherman combination is a sure, silent way of working quiet, clear streams.

# Portaging

**TO PORTAGE,** according to Webster, is the act of carrying. Boats or goods are carried overland between navigable waters along a specific route.

Portaging has been associated mainly with canoeing because special techniques and equipment have been devised for the portaging of canoes. However, portaging kayaks and inflatable boats around river obstacles is just as practical and may be a bit easier. Small rafts can be deflated and backpacked for long portages. Kayaks can be side carried without much problem since most of them weigh under 40 pounds.

Many of the methods that apply to canoe portaging also apply to other river craft as well.

### Why Portage?

There are a variety of reasons that can make portaging necessary. In order to get from one lake or pond to another, a short overland portage may be necessary if there is no water channel connecting the two bodies of

Good balance, a good carrying yoke, and strong shoulders and legs are keys to successful portaging.

→

Opposite page—One man portages while the other hauls gear. Canoe is up in front for good visibility.

Left—Young girl displays sidearm thwart portage with lightweight canoe. Below—Two-man portage for short distances to and from landings works well.

water. Sometimes a stream or channel connects two or more lakes, but the water might be impassable due to swiftness of the current, rocks, bridges, gradient, or water depth. Rather than fighting water or water obstacles, it is often deemed safer and more practical to beach the boat, stow gear on board or in backpacks and walk from one body of water to another. The distance between bodies of water, the number of portage miles, may vary from only a few yards to several miles. Some areas, like the lakes and river district of the north central United States and the Canadian provinces, are characteristically portage lakes and rivers. Portaging can be considered a very natural part of any canoe trip.

When planning a canoe trip, a paddler should realize that portaging can only be described as *work*. Long portages may be impractical. Short portages over or through extremely rough terrain may not really be worth the effort. But portages under 3 miles over relatively mild terrain can add a change of pace to an extended cruise and can be somewhat enjoyable. Portaging is basically a means to an end, offering degrees of satisfaction and adventure. Short, flat portages under a mile should not present any problems even for novices.

Aside from portaging from one lake or stream to another, portages are sometimes required to reach paddle water at the start of a trip or get to the road or pickup vehicle after the trip. In relatively unknown areas, it's a good idea to consult topographic maps to gauge the distances of portages ahead of time. Some trips have actually been ruined before they began by sore shoulders, backs and hands—paddlers who tried to bite off more than they could chew.

Portaging is also used to bypass obstacles, danger areas or difficult stretches that canoeists feel are not worth the risk or beyond their paddling abilities. Low bridges, fences, blind bends or drops, characterized by heavy current, are spots for novice and veteran alike to consider portaging. These decisions often come upon the paddler very quickly. On a new stretch of river and if in doubt, the best rule is to portage. That decision may require some extra work and loss of float time, but smart boaters will stay dry and enjoy the rest of the float. Nearly every canoeist who has progressed to the advance stage of paddling has wished, at some time or another, that he or she would have chosen portaging over "blind luck." Staying on a time schedule, keeping up with the other boats, and fear of being too cautious are flimsy reasons for not portaging. Good canoeists are good portagers.

## Portaging Techniques

Most persons, and some boaters, think of portaging as a one-man struggle with a canoe balanced on top of the shoulders. That is but one technique of portaging and, if done correctly, should not be a struggle. However, there are many ways of carrying a canoe over land. The first and most simple for very short distances is the *side carry* by one person with hands on the gun-wale at amidship and the canoe carried snugly against the hips. Frequent rest breaks will be needed, but this technique is all right for portages under 200 yards for a single person.

There are also two-, three- and four-person carries, using handholds near bow and stern with canoe righted or (with four men) in the inverted position. Two men, with their gear stowed on board and carrying light day packs, can carry a canoe a long way by taking slow, short steps and using bow and stern handholds.

Over snow and ice, a canoe or kayak can be towed like a sled. In some northern climes, lake and river water opens before all the snow has melted from the ground. Gear and paddles can be stowed in the boat and pulled by one or two persons with a bow rope of 10 or 15 feet in length. Sledding the canoe over deep, soft snow is much more practical than trying to carry it. Snowshoes help, but even then breaking through the crust is hard on legs and shoulders when carrying a boat.

A single person portage is common and when using some type of carrying yoke that evenly distributes the weight of the boat, this method works reasonably well.

An on-the-spot yoke can be made by taking two paddles and lashing them across the center thwarts. The shaft knobs can be tied on opposite sides of each other against the gunwales while the blades can be lashed to the other thwart so they overlap. The blades, with rolled up jacket or life vest as shoulder pads, ride on the portager's shoulders like a yoke while the for-

Cartopping can be a form of portaging from one lake or stream to another. Strong tie-downs are a must.

ward portion of the canoe is supported with hands on the gunwales. If a lot of portaging is predicted, commercially manufactured carrying yokes, available from most canoe manufacturers as optional equipment, are handy. Yokes, with cushioned pads angled to fit the shoulders, mount on the center thwart and can be left there, ready anytime for portaging. Paddles can be tied to the thwarts when not used as carrying yokes.

Getting the canoe onto one's back can be accomplished by positioning the canoe on its side, with the bottom of the hull facing you. Lift the boat onto your knee and then with the other hand grab the center thwart and in one continuous motion, using your knee to help lift, roll the canoe over and onto your back. By starting off with a good center of balance, at the yoke thwart, you will have little difficulty placing the cushioned pads on your shoulders. Legs should be spread to about the width of the shoulders for good balance. The front end of the canoe will be tilted upward so the boat is resting on the shoulders and supported by the arms. The portager, of course, will not be able to see overhead or to the sides, but should have a good view directly ahead when the boat is tilted. Walk with smooth, steady steps.

Coming out from under the canoe can be accomplished in a variety of ways, depending on the strength of the portager. Some paddlers bring arms in to the shoulders, slide boat forward off the carrying pads and yoke. Then, in one continuous motion, lift the boat off the shoulders, roll it over, grab the closest part of the center thwart or gunwale, and slide the canoe down off the hips and onto the ground.

Another way is to drop the downward end to the ground, bring arms in to the shoulders, lift off the pads, and rotate head and body. By pressing the canoe upward and using the arms for support, walk out from under the boat, being careful not to let it roll over and fall.

A third method of getting out from under a portaged canoe is to set the front of the boat on a limb, fence or wall and duck walk out from under the boat.

## Portage Packs

Small to medium size day packs or soft, internally framed packs make ideal portage packs. Conventional backpacks ride high enough to interfere with yoke portaging. However, they are fine for other portaging techniques. Remember that portaging is work. Gear should be limited as much as possible.

L. L. Bean of Freeport, Maine, makes a wonderful woven ash pack basket, rigid enough to carry breakable items but flexible and low-riding enough for comfort.

## Portaging Tips

Sometimes the easiest looking portage routes are not the best. Dense timber and brush can make portaging frustrating. Consult local canoeists, rangers and topographic maps for best routes. Sacrificing straight portages through dense or hilly terrain for longer routes through flatter, clearer lands is usually best.

Avoid abrupt turns or stops when portaging alone with a yoke. Hitting trees and brush with the boat can be frustrating and lead to painful wear and tear on shoulders, neck and legs. Portage slowly at your own pace.

More than one canoeist, comfortable in the boat with a pair of tennis shoes or boating moccasins, has forgotten to pack along a pair of hiking boots for portaging. Feet and ankles suffer strain when carrying a boat. A good pair of hiking boots, able to protect the feet and ankles against strain, abrasions, wet ground or snow, are as important as a good carrying yoke.

Portaging is laborious, no doubt about it. But the right equipment and know-how, along with good planning, makes it a satisfying part of the paddling experience.

# Lining

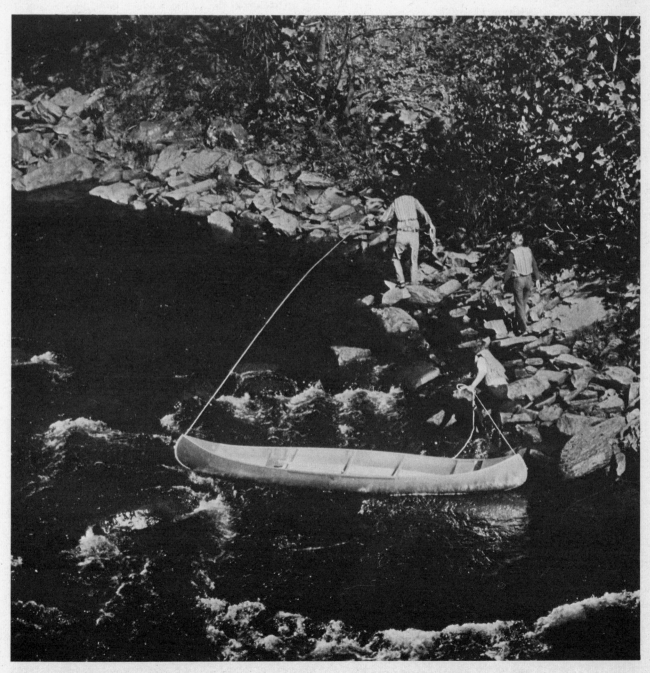

This is the standard lining technique going upstream—longer bow line than stern line.

**WHEN UPSTREAM** or downstream paddle control of canoe, kayak or inflatable boat becomes impossible because of shallow, rocky water or swift current, the boater may elect to *line* the craft and prevent injury. It is just one of many techniques a paddler has available as an alternative to negotiating impractical or dangerous waters or those beyond the abilities of the floater. Good boaters make frequent use of lining methods because they work. Uninformed beginners may not be aware of the technique or may believe that getting out of the boat and avoiding difficult stretches is not an acceptable practice. Employing the lining method often shows good judgment. Lining can be a fun alternative to portaging and a good chance to stretch the legs.

### What is Lining?

Lining is a technique most effectively used by two persons on shore by which bow and stern lines are used to "line" or guide a boat through a difficult or impassable stretch of water. One-person lining is possible with one or two ropes (manipulating each at the same time). However, two-person lining, one person slightly ahead of the bow and the other at the stern, can be the most efficient method of maneuvering a boat through a nasty stretch.

Lining can be employed either upstream or downstream. Bow and stern ropes should each be about 50 feet long and made of ¼-inch nylon or dacron rope. Be sure, before lining, that ropes are well secured to bow hooks, rings, cleats, bars or grab loops. A weak knot could lead to a damaged or lost boat. For upstream lining, the bow line is kept longer than the stern line in order to angle the boat into the current. The stern line is used for checking the angle. The distance from the liners to the boat depends primarily on the nature of the shoreline and the water. The boat can be lined when going upstream in the calmest water possible, so that it can be easily pulled and guided. Lining distance will vary as ropes are lengthened and drawn to maneuver the boat through and around obstacles.

Downstream lining requires that the bow line be kept shorter than the stern line. The short line keeps the stern headed away from the bank because of the force of the current. And the distance from liners to boat can

Another technique of lining or walking a canoe through an unfloatable passage.

Extremely steep or rocky banks can make it too tough for safe lining.

be varied by lengthening or drawing line as needed. The downstream current in combination with the ropes works the boat in or out.

### Is Lining Easier Than Portaging?

Lining can be either easier or more difficult than portaging, depending on the nature of the shoreline and the obstacles in the stream. For short stretches where gear can be kept on board, lining is usually the preferred method. If the land along the river is impractical for portaging—no clear trails and steep terrain, it is usually better to line. Where portaging routes would take the boaters away from the stream, lining might be the best technique.

On the other hand, some streams can be so full of rocks, logs or debris that lining is frustrating and next to impossible. An extremely swift current could discourage lining. Jagged, boggy, slippery, steep or meandering shorelines are often so tough to line (without falling or getting wet) that it is far better to portage. Upstream lining can be hard work pulling against the current. The longer the distance that needs to be covered, the more favorable portaging becomes.

### The Hazards of Lining

Lining a canoe along a rocky, moss-covered shore where it is difficult to stand much less tow an 85-pound boat demonstrates one of the hazards of lining. Going upstream, the bow liner although doing his share of the pulling often has the better deal. He can work further inshore, away from the slippery rocks, while the stern liner is snubbed close to the boat and nearly in the water. The importance of a pair of sturdy non-slip wading shoes or hip waders can't be emphasized enough here. Barefooting is dangerous. And shoes with little support can lead to sprains and bruises.

In regard to techniques, the main mistake that should be avoided by liners is lack of rope control (resulting ordinarily from a mix-up of signals from bow and stern men), which leads to the boat turning broadside in a heavy current and flipping. Keep the bow angled into the current and make sure it does not get too far broadside.

When some boaters give up and head home, those who use lining to get through the obstacles may be in for special treats.

# Canoe Safety

An overloaded or improperly trimmed canoe is an open invitation to capsizing or swamping.

**DIFFERENT** brands and styles of canoes have varying degrees of stability. "Goosey" might be one word to describe the raw stability of canoes. And, what manufacturers and avid canoeists describe as "good stability" may reflect instead the skill and knowledge of the canoeist. Stability is, in reality, a low center of gravity, good trim, smooth proficient stroking, and common sense. Increased canoe stability is directly proportional to increased canoeing proficiency. It is the inherent quality of the craft that begs to be balanced, controlled and made stable. A good canoeist makes a canoe good.

Because stability and balance are a challenge, like the difference between *riding* a bicycle and *operating* a car, there comes with canoeing special considerations for safety. Consider a few points.

## Swimming Ability

Can a person really enjoy canoeing if he or she cannot swim? Yes, provided that person's inability to swim has not resulted from a fear of water. Swimming, dog paddling, or back floating should be mastered before attempting to canoe. In addition, each canoeist should learn how to negotiate currents if the boat should capsize. That is, by floating on the back with legs up and out, facing downstream. In event of spilling, the canoeist should assume this position as soon as he hits the water. Like downhill skiing, the best practice is falling down. For canoeing, dunk yourself in the water first and get the feel of the current.

## Canoe Instruction

Take it! There's a wide variety of clubs, civic groups, sportmen's organizations, Boy Scouts, Girl Scouts, Red Cross, YMCA, YWCA, camps, city and state agencies that offer canoe lessons free or for a nominal charge. Lessons prevent bad habits, help overcome fears and guide novices through decisions about buying equipment of their own. Many beginner classes develop into enduring canoe clubs. And good canoeing streams are often located through classes and clubs. Instructional pamphlets and books are fine, but nothing beats the firsthand learning process with fellow novices who share a common interest and goal.

Life preservers have added some style. Most boating vests are U.S. Coast Guard approved and can be worn comfortably at all times.

## Life Preservers

Life preservers live up to their name. They save lives. Today preservers are also known as flotation jackets or vests, flotation devices, life saving devices, life jackets, competition vests, canoe vests and buoyant vests or jackets—all are labeled PFDs (Personal Flotation Devices) by the Coast Guard. Few today are *not* Coast Guard approved (for example, water skiing belts are not approved "devices"), however, make sure that any you wear are stamped or labeled "Coast Guard Approved." Also, make sure that the PFD is properly sized for the wearer; most have a weight specification included with the Coast Guard approval.

Modern vests or jackets are filled with closed cell marine foam flotation and are less bulky than the old standard, kapok or cork preservers. Quite possibly, one of the most important, yet unheralded, advances in sport boating in recent years has been the modernization of the life preserver. Why? Personal Flotation Devices are now attractive, formfitting, and comfortable. This means they can be worn at *all* times when canoeing, rather than tucked under the seats. Foam nylon shells, insulated against cold and heat, double their usefulness. They are made in men's, ladies' and child's sizes. Front zippers, side adjustments and quick release buckles make wearing vests and jackets more convenient and pleasant.

## Canoe Streams and Rivers

Safety means knowing that some streams and rivers are far beyond the skills of average canoeists. Leave heavy white water, dangerous chutes and rapids to the experts who are fully aware of the consequences of mistakes. Choose streams recom-

The most important canoe safety rule: *Wear properly fitted life jackets when afloat.*

Opposite page—Snags such as tree branches and rocks require preplanning moves and strokes far in advance. A good knowledge of strokes and life preservers are musts for white water running.

Above—Practice righting a capsized canoe *before* taking that float trip. Right—Even when swamped, canoes should have enough built-in flotation to prevent foundering.

mended for canoeing. Judge the difficulty of a stream not only by its course, obstacles and water flow, but by water temperature, wind and chill factors, and ingress and egress routes in case of emergency. Realize that the most notorious white water rivers in the country are negotiated mainly by large, commercially operated, inflatable rafts run by professionals.

### The Tip or Hit and Fall

You will, at one time or another, tip over in a canoe or hit an obstacle that forces the boat to tip over. That's why it is good to practice falling out of a canoe in a swimming pool or in a quiet stretch on a nice warm day. Make falling out of a boat a reflex movement. Several things should be kept in mind. You may want to exit and then grab the canoe to prevent it from floating away and to use the boat for flotation. As you fall, keep your hands and arms in front of your face and head to avoid being hit by the boat or obstacles in or along the river. Roll out of the boat rather than making a panicked effort to get away from it. One of the worst things is getting a foot, leg or arm trapped inside.

### Entrapment

There are more cases of fatal or injurious entrapment in kayaks than in canoes, but canoe entrap-

ment occasionally occurs. Some canoes are manufactured with cross bracing under the thwarts and seats for extra strength. However, the braces can snare a leg or foot, preventing a hasty exit. In a similar fashion, extremely low slung seats or those with shelves or braces can be death traps to a canoeist wedged or snagged underneath an overturned boat.

Sloppy bow and stern or anchor lines (the reason why good boatmen place such importance on properly coiled and placed ropes) are other hazards that can trap you under a canoe. In addition the current can cause entrapment under logs, rocks, holes and brush. If dumped from a canoe, swim or float away from obstacles that can pin you down in heavy current.

### Avoid Snags

Although some boats bounce off snags in moderate to heavy currents, a canoe usually does not. Possibly one of the most difficult maneuvers that a novice or intermediate faces in a stream is being sucked by the current into dangerous snags. Shallow water snags, such as, tree trunks, branches, rocks or brush are usually not as troublesome as those found in deep, heavy water. Safety dictates avoiding such snags by pre-planning moves and strokes far enough in advance.

## Stay With the Boat

There are times when lake canoeing or stream running that you can elect to stay with a capsized boat. On a lake, the boat can help you reach shore. On a stream, you can float through the riffles until you get to calm or shallow water to beach the canoe. In heavy water, it is often advisable to move away from the boat, which could hit or entrap you. Another alternative is to stay clear of the boat, yet retain a hold on the bow or stern rope.

## First Step Could Be The Last

In a crouching position, with hands on the gunwales, enter a canoe carefully by putting one foot near the middle of the floor, sliding the torso over the gunwales and slowly swinging the other foot in. Have a partner steady the canoe with a paddle as you enter or exit. Exiting should also be performed in low profile, one foot at a time. Stepping directly into or exiting a canoe or small boat in an upright position without any kind of handhold usually causes a capsize and discouragement.

## Proper Clothing

Dress warmly enough so that cold or chilly weather does not force you to make questionable decisions and mistakes. Cooler waterway temperatures and wind can produce cold bodies and foolish haste. Extra clothes can always be shed. Rain gear is standard equipment.

## Hypothermia

Hypothermia is caused by severe lowering of the body temperature. Body heat is lost at a faster rate than the system can replace it. Cold, wetness and wind can cause it. It's a good idea to have some idea of survival times in cold water—survival time in 30 or 40 degree water is, at best, only a few minutes without proper protection. A scuba diver's wet suit is the best precaution for cold water temperatures and weather.

# Dressing for the Occasion

Guide, Paul Crittenden, wears heavy-duty rain jacket, woolen shirt and sweater, waders and cowboy hat to protect against the elements on an early spring float.

**DICK LUDEWIG,** a friend from Cody, Wyoming, who is a superior and dedicated outdoorsman and an excellent guide, once sent me a list of "essentials" that were being mailed to all persons preparing for a week long wilderness boating-camping adventure on the southeast arm of Yellowstone Lake.

Ludewig's epistle, here in abbreviated form, is a classic.

"You feel clean in clean underwear. Bring enough so you can change each day on the trail. Throw in an extra pair for good luck. Women note—riding horseback for hours WITHOUT BRA may lead to pain not in keeping with your outdoor experience. What about long underwear? You probably won't use it unless as pajamas. (Editor's note: It's great for preventing chafed knees, thighs and buttocks on horseback trips.) However, if you feel better knowing they're along, bring a pair. Include one (1) pair of socks for each day out plus one extra pair.

"In the backcountry, we look at our shirts and slacks as protection from the elements, from insects, scrapes and snags—and as part of the system for keeping warm. Color is pleasant. We like to change shirts as the temperature climbs. When choosing your backcountry wardrobe, consider durability and comfort first. Whatever you do, don't choose the threadbare pair of cast-off slacks you use for gardening or scrubbing floors. Imagine the seat coming out 4 hours down the trail! Deep colors stay fresh appearing longer. And you won't have room to carry a change of clothes for each spatter of mud or drop of coffee."

Most commercial float outfitters, unlike Dick Ludewig, assume you know how to dress for the outdoors. It is up to you to determine the type and number of clothes to wear and pack.

Canoeing, kayaking and rafting demand sensible and appropriate clothing. A full wet suit is important for cold water or cold climate canoeing and kayaking. It is relatively cheap insurance (about $120 dollars worth) against hypothermia in case of accidental dunking.

Dressing in wool and breathable nylon according to the layer principle is necessary for early and late season boating. During the summer, however, and depending on the climate, wool can be too hot. Loose-fitting cotton is a good alternative. Wear long pants, long-sleeved shirts, and a wide-brimmed hat. Pack a pair of cut-offs or swimming suit for a mid-day dip. However, bring more clothing than you think you will actually need. Cover the body with comfortable slacks and shirts. Pack along rain gear (pants and parka) just in case and extra shirts and jackets for early morning and late afternoon when temperatures, especially on the water, have a tendency to drop fast.

I'm not going to make a list. My friend Dick Ludewig said it all. Dress for the elements. Go over-prepared. Today's good outdoor clothing is warm, practical and good looking.

Spray skirts and canoe splash cover keep paddlers dry and help prevent hypothermia.

Small day packs (below) can store extra clothes. Larger packs (left) are fine for extended float trips. A life preserver is part of proper dress.

There are times when shorts or a bathing suit permit a refreshing dip.

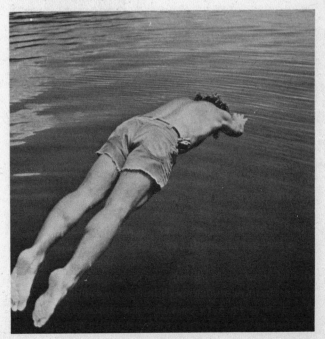

# Canoe Camping

**IT IS FALL** and the leaves have turned tawny. The day is crisp and filled with an unbelievable array of satisfying smells. Somewhere downstream campers burn logs of cedar, and an ever so slight upstream breeze carries wafts of sweet scent to my nostrils. How long has it been since I smelled the perfume of an outdoor fire?

The canoe glides ahead with a mere slice of the paddle. The water is flat and sweet, eager to please. Although at times I crave the bounce of churning white, I savor the level ride. It feels good and so do I. Oaks and trunk-to-trunk black walnuts line the banks. It is damp along the river, and a thick earthen aroma hangs heavy. Wisps of camp smoke and bottomland musk unite and form a blend so pleasurable I wish the stuff could be caught, bottled, and rationed later on in the city where I need it.

In early morning there is a stillness on the river that can be felt sharply in the chest. I know there are whitetail deer along this stretch. I've seen them. And wild turkeys and squirrels, too. They are there now along the banks, and although not in view, their eyes are penetrating. They watch me glide. And they see me as a log floating on the water and they drink. Smooth, soft and silent, boat and boatman do not scare them. It feels good to be once again a part of things natural.

This is the time of the mallard and the honker. A hen hidden on a back slough sounds a series of low, gutteral quacks. And a drake responds with an excited, high-pitched voice. After I have drifted past, the two will come together on the river.

A chorus starts somewhere off in the distance and grows in intensity at each stroke of the paddle. Soon the sounds in unison are near the river in a staggered V formation. The Canada geese are treetop high coming on fast and sure with slow, powerful wing beats and bugling notes of fall migration. As they fly over the river, their chests and necks dip and rise gracefully with each wing beat. Despite the fact that I ceased paddling and sat quietly mesmerized at their appearance, the honkers flare at my presence and angle off sharply to the east. Their nasal cries take on a panicked squeal, and they quickly put distance between us.

The sun climbing steadily through the trees sets a misty glow to the "riverscape." The breeze picks up, and the russet leaves flutter and crackle from spindly limbs. The day is blossoming bright. Gone is the filtered veil of intimate dawn. My thoughts turn to camp.

The cedar logs have burned low, and the wind that stirs the coals bellows them crackling orange. My wife Kathy and daughter Brittany are huddled close to the embers as I beach the canoe. It is the aroma of bacon and eggs now that dominates the morning air. Our tent, nestled in the oaks, drips with autumn dew, and the beagle Radar greets me with long ears and a wagging tail. The dawn float had filled my spirit, and only the return to camp could cap off a greater sense of natural living. We were together, sharing what the woods and the river had to offer. There would be times for fishing, hiking, photography and just plain talking, and for a family what more could there be together?

## The Complete Canoe Camp

Rivers and streams in almost every part of the country are avenues to the finest camping and outdoor adventure available to us today. The combination of swift, silent canoes and modern lightweight camping equipment results in comfortable, mobile outdoor living that has few equals. Depending on the size of the canoe, the number of passengers, and packing ability, the canoe camper has a choice of conventional gear or lightweight, compactable backpack gear. With the addition of ultralight fishing gear, miniature cameras, and lightweight but warm clothing, the canoe camp can be a complete and wonderful outdoor experience.

## Conventional Canoe Camp Equipment

In a 17-foot canoe, a camper can carry nearly every bit of essential camp gear. Equipment includes a modern exterior framed 8-foot × 10-foot tent, down or Dacron Fiberfill II sleeping bags with their own stuff sacks and waterproof plastic covers, and foam sleeping pads. For the outdoor kitchen, pack a gas stove, ice coolers of appropriate size to handle individual or family needs, gas lantern, and food bag with nonperishables (dehy-

Left—All is well at camp and the boats are beached for the afternoon. Below—There is good talk to be shared around the fire.

drated and freeze-dried foods and snacks), plates and utensils. The clothing bag should be stuffed with extra socks, underwear, slacks, shirts, rain gear and jackets. Everything that is essential for a comfortable, efficient camp a boater can pack. Also important is the manner in which the gear and food is packed, stowed and secured.

Individual canvas or heavy nylon stuff sacks are best for dividing up gear into stowable sizes. Everything should be bagged to keep it organized. As a further precaution against rain or spills, heavy-duty plastic garbage bags are used as outside coverings and tightly secured to make them virtually waterproof. The most common mistake canoe campers make is believing gear does not have to be tied down for flat water trips. Lash all gear to center thwarts so in case of a spill none of it will be lost. Lashing only takes a few extra minutes and is worth the extra effort.

Keep loads low and amidships unless traveling alone where some of it can be used for trim. Long items such as tent bags and poles along with fishing rods can be packed on either side of the keel line so they are out of the way. Some tents have poles that break down into numerous sections and don't take up much room. Tents should be folded into carrying bags so they fit amidships. Multi-section, break-down pack rods are much easier to stow and keep from breaking, than one or two piece rods. The heaviest items should be packed on a plastic floor cloth first and lighter gear packed on top of them. Try to keep most of the load below the gunwales. There will be times when that is impossible. When the load exceeds gunwale height, a canvas or nylon pack cover should be placed over the individual packs, tied as one large bundle, and secured to the thwarts. This keeps the lighter, top-of-the-load items from falling off and gives protection in case of bad weather or heavy water.

Good food and plenty of it is a welcome part of the canoe camping adventure.

45

Just a few of the choices a canoe camper has in the way of tents.

### Camp Food

Don't skimp on food. Dehydrated and canned foods are fine. A mixture of fresh and canned meats and vegetables offers pleasing variety. I feel the success and morale of many camps is based on the quality of food and how it is prepared. Your canoe offers enough room for a generous selection of good, nutritional foods. For packing food, items like flour, instant soups, milk, salt, and sugar can be removed from rigid, hard-to-pack boxes and double-sacked with plastic. Identify the sack since many powdered or granulated foods look alike. Cooking instructions or recipes can be cut from the box and placed in the plastic sack. A day's menu at a canoe camp might go like this:

**Breakfast**

Eggs and blueberry pancakes. An omelet made with powdered eggs hits the spot when served with bacon or sausage. A baking mix, like Bisquick, really proves its worth for drop biscuits or easy light pancakes. A real treat on the river is to add a cupful of berries (frozen blueberries work great if there are none available for picking) to a cup of baking mix. Combine milk, egg and oil with batter and pour out the cakes on a hot griddle. Serve with syrup or honey, butter and hot coffee.

That's canoe camping!

**Lunch**

Our family likes camp lunches light because they usually come at odd times after fishing or swimming. Smoked or dried sausage or salami, cheese, crackers, soup and fruit provide simple but satisfying lunches. Plenty of cold drinks or in early spring and fall hot chocolate, bouillon or coffee tops off the meal. Sweets may not be recommended nutritionally, but they can be satisfying desserts for river lunches.

**Supper**

Our favorite is fresh caught bass, trout, walleye or panfish fillets coated in a batter of egg, salt, pepper, Bisquick and beer—mixed to the consistency of pancake batter. Fillets are fried fast in hot bacon grease or oil in a skillet. They are done (flaky and light) when golden brown on each side. Top off with hush puppies (2 cups cornmeal, 1 cup flour, salt, 2 tsp. baking powder, 3 tbsp. bacon grease and chopped onion. Add enough water to make stiff dough. Roll into thumb-size pieces and fry with fish in deep fat), wow! A salad made with fresh watercress tops off the dinner. Camp meals like this are just as unforgettable, as the river camps themselves.

# Food and Water Rules

**WHEN I FIRST** received a packet of rules and regulations from the National Park Service at Canyonlands National Park in Moab, Utah, I was somewhat skeptical. "Why all the fuss?" I mumbled to myself. "There's enough paperwork here to run the army."

A request for *information* regarding boating information on the Colorado River through Cataract Canyon brought an overwhelming list of rules covering everything from personal hygiene to what food to pack along. I was miffed. "Doesn't Big Brother give us credit for any intelligence?"

It wasn't until I floated tricky sections of major western rivers and saw for myself the foolish mistakes that a lot of people made that the Park Service Rules and Regulations began to make sense. I studied accident and fatality reports which are sad testimonies to the serious consequences of "small" mistakes. Inadequate boating skills and inferior equipment were responsible for most of the unfortunate occurrences, as they are on other streams and rivers. But within the guidelines posted for major float areas in national parks across the country, a less obvious, but equally serious threat to safety and enjoyment, kept cropping up. Guidelines for the correct handling of food and water, for 2-day to 10-day trips, were constantly brought to my attention.

Whether the stream be a raging, western white waterway or a gentle, meandering Ozark stream, particular care and attention must be focused on food and water, which can be just as important as skill and good equipment for overnight or extended trips. Rafters, canoers and kayakers should be equally concerned. Improper food selection and handling or poor treatment of water can turn the best planned, best equipped river expedition into an uncomfortable mess. Bad food and water can seriously impair the physical and mental well-being of boatman, paddler and crew. Good judgment is affected. Mistakes are made and dangerous mishaps can result.

There are varying degrees of discomfort associated with the effects of bad food and/or water. But one thing is certain. Even the mild effects of diarrhea or stomach cramps weaken a person physically and detract from the enjoyment of the trip. A simple, basic knowledge of food handling rules and water treatment techniques can eliminate all problems of illness caused by bad food or water. Most of these rules are common sense guidelines that we learned as children and carry throughout our adult lives.

With helpful information supplied by the National Park Services, here is a guideline for food and water handling that can be easily followed.

### Hand Washing

Yes, out on the river hand washing is a bit more inconvenient. There're a lot of chores to be done or the fish are biting and someone forgets to put a pot of wash

The success of a float and sandbar camp is based on good food and water.

water on the fire or stove for heating. The cook merely dips his or her hands in the stream to wash the sweat and dirt off from a day's paddling. The fishermen and tent setters, having been called to dinner, find no hot water and soap and conveniently rinse their hands in the river. No hot water, no soap—totally inadequate preparation for killing germs or preventing the spread of disease. A real gamble when river running.

Shigellosis, like other types of dysentery, is transmitted fecal-orally. Hands inadequately washed, or not washed at all, can spread disease to others in a group. Food, water and equipment contaminated by infected persons are potential means of spreading disease.

Hand washing for *all* members of a float party should be established routine practice before any food is handled, before eating (including snacks), and after

Above — Food should be kept in soft or rigid coolers and eaten before spoilage. Right — Water, even from a crystal-clear stream, should be purified.

going to the bathroom. If these rules seem more stringent on a float trip than they do at home, they are meant to be. At home, the bathroom, a bed or medical attention are conveniently available. Not so on the river.

Hands should be washed with hot water and soap and dried with a paper towel. A good camping practice, as well as a good floating rule, is to keep a big pot of wash water available at all times to be heated on stove or fire. Water is transferred from the kettle to a wash pan for individual use. Wash water can be discarded away from camp, preferably dumped on sandy soil or dirt, away from the river bank.

### Pre-Trip Illness

If illness like diarrhea, hepatitis or flu is diagnosed before a trip begins, that person, rather than risking the chance of infecting other floaters, should not make the trip.

## Food Handling

The Park Service says the less food that is handled, the better. Trip cooks, or those persons alternating as cooks, should do the food handling and only after they have thoroughly washed their hands.

All foods should be wrapped in suitable, non-absorbent material, except canned or prepackaged items. Plastic wrap or plastic bags qualify. Some foods, like lettuce for instance, are not usually cooked and can harbor disease. Lettuce and other vegetables should not be allowed to lie for any length of time out of the cooler or directly in the ice melt at the bottom of the cooler.

Ice should be safe to use in drinks. It should be made at home or purchased from a licensed ice manufacturer or commercial-type ice maker.

Fresh meats are likely to spoil when not chilled and pork or chicken are the most vulnerable of the meats. Beef is better to use. Frozen food should not be thawed at temperatures in excess of 45 degrees Fahrenheit.

## Refrigeration

There are many good ice chests or soft ice bags on the market that feature sturdy insulation and nonabsorbent interior shell material. On extended floats you may need several ice chests—one for meats and produce, another for beverages, and a third for storing extra ice and fish.

Ice chests and bags should have drainage plugs to minimize ice melt in the bottom of the chest. And they should be easy to clean. Perishable items like mayonnaise, fish products, and sandwich spreads are better purchased in small containers so they can be used in one or two days.

## Paper Plates, Bowls and Cups

There are arguments pro and con for the use of disposables. Some call them a waste of natural resources. For float tripping, single-service eating/drinking gear is extremely handy, eliminates dish washing, and in the case of poor washing or rinsing, safeguards against the chance of uncomfortable cramps or diarrhea. Plastic knives and forks are also recommended. Disposable items should be burned completely, where burning or fires are permitted. Otherwise they should be packed out in large, heavy plastic garbage bags.

If stainless steel or aluminum dishes and utensils are used, clean them in a chlorine solution in which 2 teaspoons or one capful of chlorine bleach is added to each gallon of wash water. Completely immerse dishes and utensils for at least 60 seconds in the solution and allow to air dry after removal.

## Disinfection of Drinking Water

Using household chlorine bleach, add 8 drops to each gallon of raw water. Iodine from a first aid kit can be used, mixing 20 iodine drops with a gallon of raw water.

Cooking fresh foods over open fire insures good spirits and a happy camp.

When halazone tablets are used, follow the directions on the label. Or, boil water vigorously for at least 2 minutes.

Whether chlorine or iodine is used, mix the water and drops thoroughly by stirring or shaking. Let the water stand for 30 minutes before drinking. Chlorine is a gas and after it has done its job will dissipate in about 30 minutes, giving little or no taste.

## Water Storage

Water storage containers should have a closed top that can be tightly sealed. The container itself should be smooth and clean. Commercially sold water jugs or 5-gallon plastic containers can serve the purpose for water storage.

## When to Purify Water

Even the most remote waters of the country are subject to some kind of contamination or pollution. Major float rivers, not coming directly from the untampered high country, contain water that needs to be purified.

Unless packing your own water from home, it's a good idea to purify *all* water, regardless of how pure or clear the stream appears. Purification can be done in advance so that quantities of water are ready for drinking, cooking or washing.

# First Aid on the Water

BEHIND THE subject of first aid and first aid kits lurks the suspicion that too much emphasis is wasted on preparing for the negative. Why not simply look forward to the good things surrounding an outdoor adventure?

I can get boyishly excited over the prospects of floating a new stretch of river or the thought of deep, mysterious trout holes downstream. But adhesive tape, gauze, snake bite kits, calamine lotion and all the itching, scratching, swelling and pain that accompany these tools of pessimism never stir me much.

After all, first aid kits are boxes that you never can find when you need them. They always work their way to the bottom of the boat where they become filled with water and coated with grime. When the need for the first aid kit arises, opening the lid of the box often reveals a hopelessly soggy mess of bandage, gauze and punctured ointment tubes. Which just goes to prove the utter uselessness of first aid kits.

From a practical viewpoint, the first aid kit is a box of *insurance*. Good ones are rather heavy and take up precious storage space. Small kits get lost. So does it pay to carry a lot of insurance? The answer is *yes*. The fanciest first aid kit is only as good as the working condition it is in and the ability of its owner to find it quickly and be able to effectively use the tools and medicines contained therein.

## When to Pack a First Aid Kit

The idea that first aid kits are only needed on extended float trips or through difficult stretches is a foolish one. Whether the trip be a 3-hour fishing trip or an overnighter, the very nature of river floating is reason enough to have a good, working first aid kit on board.

It is not so much the idea that a lot of bad things can happen on float trips, but rather the degree of isolation associated with floating. Even near metropolitan areas, the meandering course a stream takes can be quite inaccessible to roads, highways, houses and help. Some rivers are characterized by high canyon walls along their courses which prohibit access to areas

where help can be sought. For this reason, distance or difficulty rating should not be the sole determining factor in first aid consideration and preparation. The fact that immediate first aid can be given when needed can prevent discomfort and possible serious consequences later on. With some basic preparations, float trips that might be otherwise spoiled by minor ailments or injuries will only be temporarily interrupted.

## The Best Kit for Your Float

The size of your boat with its space and weight restrictions dictates the type of first aid kit you will have on board.

In a survey conducted by the National Park Service and the Interagency Whitewater Committee, which includes river managers and guides, various first aid kits were reviewed and evaluated. Major and minor first aid kits varied from area to area, with the degree of isolation being the apparent reason for the size of kits. Major kits ranged in size from 15 to 40 items; minor kits, from 10 to 15 items; and standard kits ranged somewhere in between these extremes.

The size of the kit is not as important as its contents. The inclusion of the necessity items is vital for major, standard and minor kits alike. The geographical characteristics of the river, along with inherent insect or reptile pests, and such nemeses as poison ivy, oak and sumac should also be considered when determining sufficient quantities of various medications.

## Basic Kit Instruments

A pair of medium size *scissors* is needed for cutting tape. A *razor* with extra blades is handy for removing hair before taping. *Tweezers* remove splinters. *Safety pins* can be used for mending and securing triangular bandages. A package of *cotton swabs* can be used for cleaning lacerations, eyes, and ears. For long trips an *inflatable splint* can be added.

## Dressings

A supply of *Band-aids* in medium and large sizes for lacerations should be kept in their own container inside

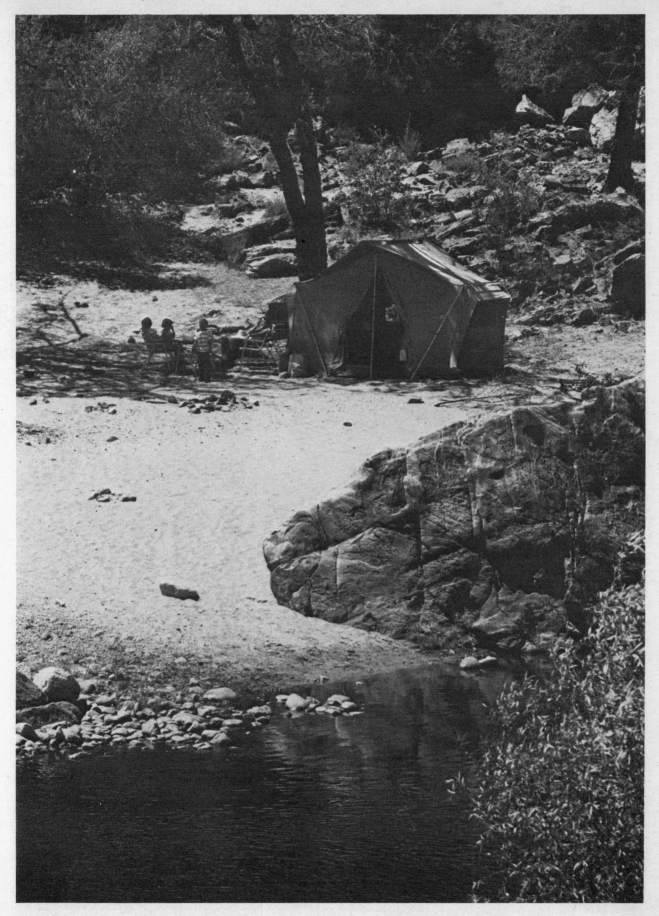

Minor injuries, requiring basic first aid attention can occur on the water or in camp.

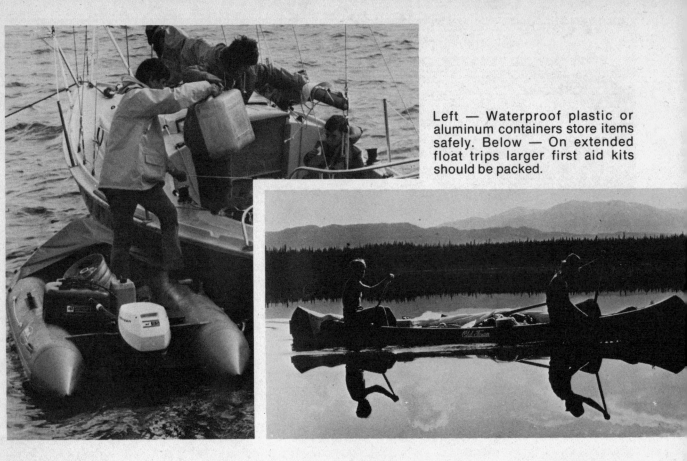

Left — Waterproof plastic or aluminum containers store items safely. Below — On extended float trips larger first aid kits should be packed.

the kit. *Butterfly Band-aids* in various sizes help close lacerations. An *elastic bandage* 2 or 3 inches wide is needed for sprains. Be certain to follow the wrapping instructions that come with the bandage to guard against blocking circulation. A couple of rolls of 2-inch *adhesive tape* secures *sterile gauze pads* or flats for large and small wounds. And several rolls of 2-inch *roller gauze* hold the gauze pads in place before taping.

### Medicinal Relief

*Aspirin*, or aspirin substitute, relieves pain or headaches. *Antacid tablets* alleviate indigestion. A bottle of *calamine lotion* soothes poison ivy or insect bite itching. Some sort of *pain killer* is advisable on long trips.

### How to Prevent Problems

A good first aid kit can solve a multitude of discomforts and minor injuries. That's why commercial floaters ordinarily carry kits that include not only basic gear and medicines, but also other items to cover almost any "field treatable" discomfort or injury in the book.

Most problems on a float trip can be prevented. Here's how. *Insects*, including mosquitoes, chiggers, bees and wasps can cause aggravating discomfort. Regardless of the season, pack along enough insect repellent to ward off insects before they swarm. New bugproof repellent jackets have proved effective, along with several brands of repellent lotion that is applied to exposed skin. Long pants, long-sleeved shirts and jackets are natural repellents. Headnets and gloves may be required in some northern areas where mosquitoes and flies are ferocious biters, and chemical repellents are ineffective.

Chiggers, especially bad in the Midwest and South, can be discouraged by liberally dousing powdered sulphur on skin areas where clothing is snug, such as ankles, waist, armpits and knees.

For overnight float camps, tents with sewn-in floors and nylon screening can prevent bites. Camp away from the water and if possible at a higher elevation to eliminate some insect problems.

Although a few bee and wasp stings are unavoidable, use some care when stopping for shore lunch or camp. Exercise caution and be alert for beehives. Look before sitting down on the ground. Floundering around at dusk or in the dark for firewood is a good way to pick up insect stings and bites.

*Snakes* can also be avoided by using caution along water areas where rattlesnakes or water moccasins (cottonmouths) are known to reside. Canyon areas bordering rivers can be especially lively with rattlers during spring, summer and fall months. Walk with care, especially during the early morning and late afternoon of summer days. Be careful where you place feet and hands. Carry a good snake bite kit in your first aid kit and know how to use it. By wearing leather hiking boots that cover the ankle or waders when fishing, the lower

Below — Headnets prevent annoying and serious bites from insects—sometimes they are the only means of relief. Right—Prevention eliminates many problems—such as drying your sleeping bag to avoid spending the following night in a damp bag.

leg, most often hit by poisonous snakes, can be protected. Be especially careful while gathering firewood not to probe in brush or under logs with your hands. Instead, use a long stick to shake brush or roll the log over first. Never trust a rock or log in snake country.

An overnight or extended float trip is no place to begin the sun tanning process. *Sunburning* often results and nothing can be more aggravating than rowing or paddling with painfully hot arms. Resist the sunning temptation or limit yourself to an hour. For face and arms, apply suntan lotion or zinc oxide sun screen. A sunburn relief lotion, like Solarcaine, can help but why let the problem develop in the first place? Mild to severe sunburning is one of the most common first aid problems on float trips and results in a wide range of discomforts from nausea and diarrhea to chills, burning skin and blisters. Sunburning ironically is the easiest problem to prevent.

### Food and Drink Intake

Proper food and drink handling is a habit that seasoned floaters get into early. Severe stomach cramps, nausea, vomiting and diarrhea are especially uncomfortable symptoms on float trips. Whether on your own float or on a commercial float, never take it for granted that the food and water are "alright." Check on it.

### Hats, Rain Gear and Sleeping Bags

Hats and rain gear are indeed first aid tools. They prevent a good number of on-stream ailments. Wide-brimmed western hats or baseball caps, for example, cut the glare of reflected sun, which can "burn" the eyes. They also prevent sunburned face and scalp. As a result, headaches and eye soreness can be reduced significantly simply by wearing hats that shield the sun.

Sudden rain squalls drench clothes and skin without the protection of *rain jackets and pants*. Chilling and colds result. Pack rain gear at all times and have it handy on board. Much of the need for aspirin or antihistamines can be reduced by wearing rain gear, warding off wet or damp clothing and staying warm.

Some commercial float outfitters provide sleeping bags upon request. It is better to bring your own *warm* bag with its own stuff sack and protective plastic covering (plus the outfitter's waterproof boat bag) and keep the bag dry. Cold or wet bags lead to insufficient rest, colds and bad attitudes.

### How and Where to Store First Aid

Store first aid instruments, medicine and ointments in a single container made of wood, aluminum or heavy duty plastic that is waterproof and equipped with strong latches for positive opening and closing. There are a number of good places to store the kit—fishing tackle box, food bag, clothing bag or flotation-cargo bag. With a piece of masking tape, mark the bag where the first aid kit is located. Keep the kit handy near the top of the duffel.

# The Nature Float

**HARNESS** the stream to your spirit. Take to your heart the flavor of living current. Inhale into citified lungs the rich aroma of bottomland vapor. You are alive. And the stream is a silver thread that curls its way through a magic land. The forest glitters. The oaks stand naked. The pines are forever green and overbearing.

When you communicate with nature from the silent, motorless drift of a float boat, you are on equal terms with her. Part of the river; part of the land that borders her. You need neither rod nor reel for true joy. There will be enough of that. And the quest for white water with its instant thrill of tumultuous ecstasy is not of immediate importance. You are alone with a peaceful river, and the world is full of things natural and wild. There is special river joy. For in the world of diminishing natural purity, every floating river is naturally pure. And you, the nature floater, are equally and bountifully blessed.

Natural water is, and always will be, a magnet for nature and wildlife. As the desert oasis draws animals, birds and vegetation, so does the float stream. Even those great rivers that bear the crowded cities of today retain a wildness about them that countless civilized pressures have failed to suffocate. The degree of wildness, the quality of nature, varies considerably. But it is there for those who seek it—from the often harassed Ohio to the dammed, once-free Snake. The serpentine courses roll on and as long as they do, we can garner their natural treasures.

Canoes, inflatables, johnboats, and wooden double-enders serve the nature floater well. And for the sheer thrill of floating "through" nature, kayaks do the job. Consider current speed when choosing a suitable craft. Canoes are great for slow to moderate currents. Inflatables, with built-in water drag, are better suited to moderate and fast water. Johnboats are fine in moderate current speeds.

Choice of craft is a matter of taste and individual needs. However, stability, maneuverability and safety are important considerations. A boat that demands constant attention may not be the best for nature obser-

vation. A boat that speeds a floater through an area with little or no time to study the surroundings could be the wrong choice. Or a boat that is sluggish and hard to paddle or row on long, smooth stretches can be more work than fun. There is no perfect boat for all waters. Choose a float boat according to the type of water you will be floating most often. A good way to find out which float craft is the best for your needs is to rent several different types before buying.

With a float craft, you have the foundation for exciting, close nature observation. Basic equipment can be as simple as your eyes, ears, nose and hands. That's really all you need. But you have the option of making your communion with nature as simple or as complex as you see fit. Add a pair of binoculars, and the views of nature can be intimate. You can record findings in a small notebook. Field guides to birds, flowers, trees, insects, reptiles, and mammals aid in identifying your sightings. Select field guides that are localized to your area or geographic zone.

Nature or wildlife photography is a wonderful bonus to nature floating. Regardless of whether the camera gear is simple or elaborate, the floater has several distinct advantages in capturing good nature shots on film. Most shots can be taken directly from the float craft. Birds and animals are spooked less by floaters than they are by persons approaching on foot. Animals and birds are concentrated along rivers which fill their water, food, and shelter requirements. Because of the silent approach, floating photographers often catch deer, raccoons, squirrels, and waterfowl in natural, undisturbed moods. And this aspect alone makes the difference between good wildlife shots and great ones. Quite a few of today's top-notch professional wildlife photographers use the rivers and float boats to get their best shots.

The 35mm SLR (single lens reflex) system is probably the best all-around camera body and lens combination for float boat photography. Equipped with a normal (55mm), wide-angle (21 or 28mm), or telephoto (200mm, 300mm, or 70-210mm zoom) lens, the photographer can handle almost any photographic situation

Left — Boaters can be treated to doe/fawn scenes like this. Below — Common sight along float rivers — waterfowl of all kinds.

Above — Many streams are clear enough to permit underwater observation. Right — Quiet float brought close-up of moose.

Above — Nature surrounds the floater who takes the time to look and appreciate. Right — Ideal protection for camera is foam-lined and compartmented Shutterpack Case.

along the river. Perhaps the most versatile lens would be a telephoto zoom. However, the distinct disadvantage to the system is that it is not waterproof. Within a securely closed plastic bag, the system can be protected from moisture damage. But, by keeping the camera locked in such a bag, good shots are often missed.

There are several alternatives. A nature floater, interested more in capturing good photos than in a fast, thrilling ride, can choose the more stable inflatable or johnboat as opposed to the less stable canoe. But a good canoeist is less apt to take a dunking and can with confidence pack along an expensive SLR system. For the average floater, photography and canoeing blend together best in slow to moderate currents.

Another alternative is the underwater camera housing. Adjustable to fit a variety of camera bodies and lenses, it can be used not only for underwater photography during a float but also as a precautionary measure when the chance of tipping or taking in water exists. The special waterproof housing, of course, can be rendered useless if the camera is lost in murky or deep water. A short shock cord, secured to camera housing and boat, prevents accidental loss. For more information on waterproof camera housings write: Ikelite Underwater Systems, 3303 North Illinois Street, Indianapolis, Indiana 46208.

The Nikonos II is an underwater 35mm camera with a special housing that makes it waterproof. Light and compact, it can be worn around the neck for quick shots. The addition of an elastic belly or chest strap, that you make yourself, holds the camera comfortably in place when paddling or rowing. In the event of a dunking, it keeps the camera safely against the body. The Nikonos II takes lenses of 15mm, 28mm, 35mm and 80 mm. The disadvantage to the system for wildlife photography is the limitation that the 80mm lens puts on the photographer. For wildlife close-ups, a 200mm is more suitable. Equipped with the 80mm lens, the photographer has to work harder for an action shot that is relatively routine with the 200mm. The Nikonos II is a good choice though, and close-ups are possible through careful, quiet floating where the photographer stalks and surprises wildlife.

Whether the photographer employs the instant photography of a Pronto SX-70 (which is a fun camera on a float trip) or the compact simplicity of an Instamatic, packing a camera along, despite the chance of accidental dunking, is always worth the effort.

## Nature Along the Banks

Trees, shrubs, plants, wildflowers, insects, and reptiles are found in abundance along most rivers. Observation of these smaller, less obvious forms of nature on the river banks may not be as dramatic as the sighting of a deer, heron, or turkey. But by taking the time to stop, observe, and investigate, new information and surprises emerge. Even a few unexpected bonuses, like the joy of discovering a patch of scrumptious morel mushrooms or a floating bed of tangy watercress, are fairly common to unhurried floaters.

## Observing Aquatic Life

With or without the use of an underwater face mask, the floater, depending on water clarity, has a chance to observe fish life, aquatic insects and plants, muskrats, beaver, otter, frogs, turtles and water snakes. All the activity is by no means confined to the banks. While the best on-land observation is usually in the early morning hours when wildlife is on the move, the finest underwater viewing comes when the sun is straight up and filters like a torch through the water. The slower the pace, the greater the opportunity of observing aquatic life—often the most interesting forms of nature.

## Tracks, Signs, and Calls

The float stream attracts all forms of wildlife to its banks. Even though observation of birds and animals is a special treat, the tracks, signs, and calls of wildlife that may not be in view of the floater make for fascinating study themselves. A majority of wildlife is nocturnal, hunting, feeding and watering under the protection of darkness. There is a special thrill involved with investigating and determining the freshness of the tracks of a raccoon that came to the water's edge during the night in search of snails. Equally as exciting is spotting the velvet rub of a whitetail deer on a tree trunk or rock in late summer.

The sounds of nature, during the stillness of a quiet float, take on distinctive meaning. The throaty call of the bullfrog. The delicate peeps of mallard ducklings. The cry of a red-tailed hawk. All these calls are magnificently clear and thrilling on the river. There are good books available on track, sign, and call identification. The *Peterson Field Guide Series* is excellent. *A Field Guide to Animal Tracks* by Olaus J. Murie is another fine book.

## Best Seasons and Times

In nature, May and June are months of birth, rebirth, and renewal, which are fascinating times to ride the river. But heavy snow or rain runoff during spring or early summer can make floating impractical and often dangerous. Low runoff and a dry spring make for ideal floating conditions for exploring the river world and new, fresh nature.

In terms of the nature float, summer is a fine time, but autumn is better. Nature is preparing for the winter ahead, and creatures are busy. Fall colors are breathtaking. Where rivers do not freeze, winter floating can be beautiful and completely different from mild-weather river running. Early morning and late afternoon hours are best for wildlife observation. Whatever the time, the nature float is extremely satisfying and the slower the pace, the more memorable it can be.

# Hunting from Canoes

**IF YOU ARE** a hunter and delight to the silent, swift stalk for game birds and animals, perhaps there is no finer, more relaxing way to hunt than by boat.

Canoes and inflatable rafts make excellent hunting boats because they blend in with the natural scheme of the river. Both types of craft are light enough to be portaged or carried, launched and taken out almost anywhere.

### The Hunting Spirit

Canoeing or rafting enkindles the hunting spirit. The magic of a misty October river sets the mood. More than the shooting, the spirit and tradition of float hunting attracts river hunters. The ingredients of both sports settles deep in the minds and bodies of persons steeped in outdoor tradition. Feel the mist on your stubbled beard. Smell the perfume of damp October leaves as they lie still and soggy beneath clusters of pecans and black walnuts. Dip the paddle into still, gray water. Look to the russet leaves and breathe in pure river spirit. Gone are the things of city worry. Are you really reborn? No doubt. Look at the worn stock of your river gun. It has given you so many good hours. And the boat. Watch it knife through the morning river as if knowing full well that game waits around the next bend. This is where you want to be, and you hope that both the day and the feeling never end.

### Hunting From Canoe or Raft

Canoes or inflatables are access tools for hunting. They can take the hunter comfortably and silently through lands where game abounds and on waters where ducks and geese may be resting. Boats open up areas that may otherwise be inaccessible because of the lack of roads or lands that are blocked by private holdings.

The boat hunter has several things in his favor. He is able to float and paddle into good areas without spooking game. Foot hunters, on the other hand, unless they are capable stalkers and have moist ground and the wind in their favor, often spook game before they see it. It is often possible to get within good shooting range,

Large concentrations of geese congregate along rivers and marshes in some areas.

both for shotgunning and rifle, by keeping a low profile and drifting as naturally as a log floating downstream.

### Game on and Along the River

Rivers are magnets for certain species of game because they provide water, food and cover for game birds, animals and migratory waterfowl. Quite naturally then, a lot of game can be concentrated along certain stretches of river. This gives the boat hunter an advantage.

The congregation of ducks, geese and huntable shorebirds is dependent on the type of river and its proximity to major and minor flyways and resting areas. The season and weather conditions are also important factors. Waterfowl ordinarily use potholes, marshes and ponds for food and cover before freeze-up and utilize rivers later on in the season. However, in heavily hunted refuge areas, ducks and geese use rivers as resting areas throughout the season. The closer the river to the shooting area, the better the chances for boaters. Rivers are used as minor flyways early and late in the day. Small ponds, back eddies and sloughs off the main river are likely spots for jumping ducks and geese. Boaters can often spot good areas from the river, beach the boats and proceed on foot.

Hunting for gray and fox squirrels can be excellent along midwestern, southern, north central and eastern streams where squirrels have plenty of cover and likely food sources. Oak, hickory and beach trees are squirrel favorites. Both gray and fox squirrels can be extremely wary. Beaching the boat and sitting still for 15 or 20 minutes, while watching a promising oak or hickory

Left — The canoe can get you into prime hunting areas fast. Above — Deer is a prime target for silent, careful stalker.

patch, will often turn up plenty of squirrels. However, slow steady drifting through likely areas can yield good close shots from the boat too.

An extremely effective method of hunting whitetail deer in the East or mule deer in the West is floating for them early in the morning and late afternoon. They water at least once a day, and if a floater is quiet and motionless, good shots under 50 yards are possible. The slow, silent stalk by boat is a tremendous advantage because bucks are taken off guard. A boat may be the most practical and efficient way of hunting dense cover where on-land stalking would only drive deer to another area.

In states like Wyoming, Alaska and the Canadian provinces, boat hunting can be very successful for other species of big game such as elk and moose.

Hunters should check the hunting regulations for boat hunting in their state. Waterfowl, for instance, can be hunted from boats in most states provided the boat is not propelled by a motor at the time of shooting.

Ordinarily, a canoe can be used for safe, practical hunts on streams of slow to moderate currents. Inflata-

Quiet floating for big game often produces close shots at deer.

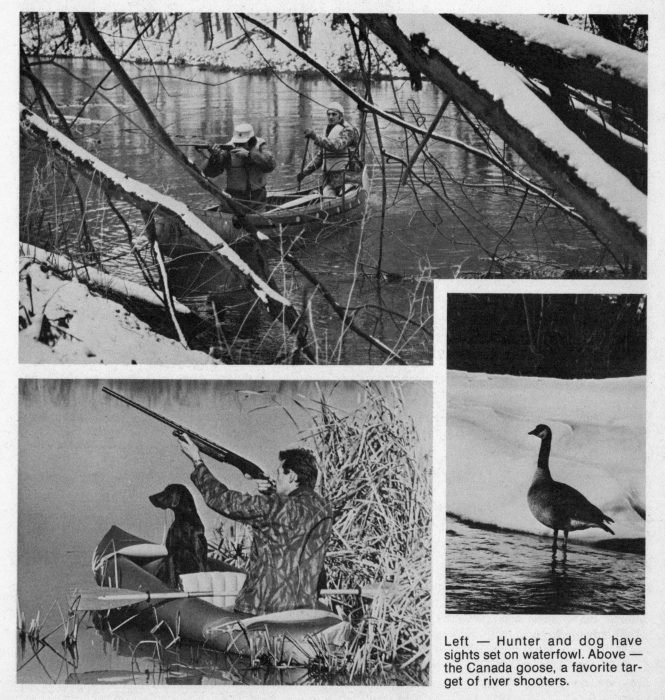

Left — Hunter and dog have sights set on waterfowl. Above — the Canada goose, a favorite target of river shooters.

Boats painted dull brown or green colors are fine for waterfowl.

ble boats are better suited to swifter streams where greater stability is desired. Generally speaking, the slower streams are better suited for waterfowl and squirrels. Consequently, a canoe would be the best choice—far easier to propel and maneuver through the long, flat stretches.

Canoes can be purchased with a brown or "dead grass" color that camouflages them when floating or used as blinds for ducks and geese. Rubber boats in gray or black are better than bright colored rafts for hunting. However, any canoe or inflatable can be fitted with a camouflage cover that can be made at home and custom fitted to the boat. Camouflage netting or nylon material can be purchased at military surplus stores or sporting goods departments and used to make a quick, effective floating blind. Paddles and oars can be painted dull colors for further camouflage effectiveness.

### Special Precautions

Cold weather and water temperatures are likely to prevail during most hunting seasons. A wise added precaution is a wet suit. Worn under loose fitting outer garments, the wet suit not only provides warmth, it is extra insurance in the event of capsizing. Canoe hunters in northern climates should consider the wet suit standard equipment.

Shooting from canoes or inflatables is not as tricky as it sounds, provided a low center of gravity is maintained. The shooter should be well anchored and have adequate control over his shotgun or rifle. As with hunting from a duck blind, shooters must swing and shoot only in their area of fire. In a boat, be especially careful of your partner in the bow or stern.

Keep shotgun or rifle within easy reach and protected from moisture, sliding, falling and banging by a tarp or piece of inch-thick foam that can be used to cushion it. Problems often develop when guns are out of reach and game is sighted. Desperate efforts to get to the gun in time for a shot could result in a dunking. *Never should the hunter keep a shotshell or cartridge in the chamber.* Ammunition can be stored in the magazine of the rifle or shotgun safely or carried in an easy-to-reach pocket for quick loading.

### Clothing

If it is cold in your neighborhood during hunting season, chances are it will be a bit cooler on the river. Rowing and paddling produce warmth. If you are not paddling, and a good duck hunting day is upon you (wind, rain and/or snow), be glad that you brought along more clothes than you thought you really needed. Extra jackets, sweaters, socks, gloves and caps can be stored in a small rucksack.

Foul weather gear, consisting of rain parka and pants (usually camouflaged for waterfowl hunters), is standard hunting equipment and should never be left behind even on days that start bright and sunny.

I have found one of the best all-around *boat hunting* boots to be the Maine hunting boot, sold by mail order from L.L. Bean, Freeport, Maine 04032. With rubber bottoms and leather tops, the Bean boot is lightweight and very comfortable. Two pairs of woolen socks can be worn or a sheepskin-leather inner-sole can be ordered extra from Bean. Keeping the feet warm is vital to the warmth of the entire body and enjoyment of the hunt.

Plenty of hot drinks and food, in addition to warm clothing, replenish energy and spark the spirit. There is no finer outdoor adventure than using a canoe or inflatable to get where the game is.

# Timetables and Rating Systems

**MORE FLOATING** experiences have been dampened by inaccurate or false float time information and difficulty ratings. Stories about "spending the night on the river" and "doing enough paddling to last a lifetime" travel fast in floating circles. Difficulty ratings have scared away some boaters too, especially the tales of supposedly flat, smooth "beginner" stretches of river that turned into frothy white water, sucking currents, and an obstacle course of rocks.

The blame, I suppose, could be traced back to the floaters themselves for not digging into the river structure a bit more thoroughly. But unfortunately, the river challenge for one may not be the same for another. The float speeds of different river boats vary. Wind conditions are factors. High and low water levels definitely make a difference in float speed (travel time from one point to another). And then there is the simple case of bad or outdated information.

Unless times and distances are recorded in writing by those actually floating the river and exact river and weather conditions noted, information can vary considerably. River guide and navigation books can virtually be deemed useless (and sometimes a hazard in themselves) when they are not accurately updated each year. Some rivers, especially the untamed giants of the west, are constantly changing their course. While obstacles, like fallen trees, dead-end water braids, and fences may disappear during one season, others take their place seemingly overnight. New channels develop; old ones lead to time-devouring portages.

What is the best floating timetable to follow?—your own. Start with rough estimates. Take careful precautions on a new stretch and add more time than is prescribed. After the float, log your findings according to: 1. time started; 2. number and duration of stops; 3. float craft used (canoe, johnboat, inflatable); 4. water conditions (high, medium, low); and 5. stream difficulty (fast, moderate, slow). A small, pocket-size notebook can serve as a handy journal for your particular craft and pace. That's the best guide for you.

Here are some facts to remember. Canoes and kayaks can be classified as *fast* float craft. The majority of published timetables for various floats are set according to the float speed for recreational canoeing and not necessarily for fishing and floating. Canoes and kayaks are the least affected by winds, and they handle well in long, flat stretches of water.

Aluminum, fiberglass and wooden johnboats, rowboats, prams, double-enders and McKenzie boats can generally be considered *average* speed floaters. Most guides and fishermen base their times made with these craft. They are considerably slower than canoes and kayaks and more affected by head winds. During long, flat stretches of water, the boats can be burdensome.

Rubber inflatables, because they feature built-in water drag, can be classified as *slow* float boats—often a blessing to fishermen working swift streams where drag allows more time to hit likely holes where lunker fish hide. The slightest head wind will slow a rubber boat down considerably.

Some rivers become treacherous during high water levels.

River ratings are proportional to water temperature. As the temperature drops below 50 degrees Fahrenheit, the difficulty rating for a given stretch of water goes up by at least one class.

## Difficulty Ratings

A more reliable guide, and one that is more generally accepted as a reference for float fishermen and canoeists alike, is based on a rating system table from one to six; the larger the number, the more difficult and dangerous the stream.

Ratings are based on criteria consisting of current speed; water obstacles; grade or fall of the water (from flat stretches to rapids and white water to dropoffs and falls); stream course (relatively straight or meandering); portages; diversion dams; or low water areas.

There are very few rivers whose entire length can be categorized under one classification. In other words, correctly defined, most rivers fall under several different ratings.

When considering river difficulty rating, evaluate your ability and the worthiness of your craft. Try to avoid the mistake of accepting the information of unknowledgeable sources as final criteria for going ahead with a float. Check as many information sources as possible for current information; take a guided scenic or fishing float on the stretch before making your own; or personally inspect known trouble spots by car or foot before putting your boat in the water.

A difficulty rating system is only as good as the agency or individual who rates it. Make sure the rating variables fall in line with your skills and equipment.

The American White Water Affiliation has established a couple of different river rating systems that can be used as general references. It is widely known that most accidents occur when boatmen attempt to negotiate water that is more demanding than their skills, knowledge and experience can justify. Most of us, however, are quick to accept a challenge, and sometimes we are "blinded" by pride in our boating and outdoor skills. Canoeists, kayakers and rafters should learn to frankly and honestly evaluate their own skills as well as the difficulty of water to be floated.

Generally speaking, Class I and II rivers can be run in open canoes. Some Class III rivers are suitable for open canoes if time is allowed for emptying water from the boat. Any class of river may change according to the amount of river runoff and the depth of water. Water temperatures below 50 degrees Fahrenheit should be considered at least one class more difficult because of the potential hazard in event of capsizing.

**Class I**—Very Easy stretch for the practiced beginner. Waves are small, regular and passages are clear. Usually gentle sand or dirt banks, with some possible artificial difficulties like bridge abutments or a few small riffles.

**Class II**—Easy stretch for intermediates. Rapids are of medium difficulty. Passages are clear and wide. Some low ledges. Spray covers might be useful. Some maneuvering is required.

Left — In addition to difficulty ratings for streams, there is an ability rating for boaters. Below left — Rapids are gauged according to swiftness and obstacles. Below right — A timetable is established by the type of craft, river speed and how many stops will be made.

**Class III**—Medium difficulty stretch for experienced boaters. There are numerous high, irregular waves. There are rocks, eddies, and rapids with passages that are clear, though they can be narrow and require expertise in maneuvering. Inspection before making the run is necessary in some areas, and spray skirt or splash cover is necessary.

**Class IV**—Difficult stretch for highly skilled boaters with several years of experience. Should be with an organized group of boaters for this run. There are long rapids and powerful, irregular waves. Dangerous rocks and boiling eddies are common. Passages are difficult, and inspection is a must. Powerful and precise maneuvering is required, and spray skirt or splash cover is essential. Conditions along these stretches make rescue difficult in case of trouble and *all* kayakers should be able to Eskimo Roll.

**Class V**—Very difficult stretch that is run by teams of experts. There are extremely long, difficult and violent rapids that follow each other almost without interruption. Plenty of obstacles, big drops, violent current and very steep gradient. Shore scouting and planning is essential, but extremely difficult because of the terrain. Because rescue conditions on this stretch are extremely difficult, mishaps can and do often lead to death.

**Class VI**—Extremely difficult stretch that is run by teams of experts. Nearly impossible stretch to run and very dangerous. Even for teams of experts, favorable water levels and close study and careful planning are needed for success.

At various times of the year, and different water levels, either through natural conditions such as rain or snow runoff or dam (impoundment) water releases, difficulty ratings can change on various stretches of

Class VI Rivers should be run only by teams of experts in appropriate craft.

river. These variances should be considered, in addition, to the classifications already listed.

**L (Low)**—Less than acceptable level for satisfactory paddling.

**M (Medium)**—Normal for rivers of slight gradient, but less than enough water for good passage in a steeper river.

**MH (Medium High)**—Higher than normal. Enough water to provide passage over ledges and through boulder gardens. This is the best level for some of the more difficult river sections.

**H (High)**—The river is full, and the water heavy. Covered boats are necessary on most rivers; some large rivers are at a dangerous level.

**HH (High-High)**—Very heavy water makes for complex and powerful hydraulics. Even rivers of moderate gradient can become dangerous.

**F (Flood)**—Abnormally high water. Extremely powerful effects with debris on the surface. Not for boating of any kind.

### Rate Yourself (Honestly) as a Paddler

Some boating clubs have various rating systems for members so that members can be matched to various stretches of water. This is a good, general guide to follow in rating your own abilities.

*Class I*—You are a beginner who knows all the basic strokes and can handle a boat competently in smooth water.

*Class II*—You are a novice who can effectively use all basic white water strokes in the kayak, or in both bow and stern areas of a canoe. You can read water and negotiate easy rapids with confidence.

*Class III*—You are an intermediate who can negotiate rapids requiring complex maneuvering. You know how to use eddy turns and basic bow-upstream techniques. In the bow or stern of a double canoe, single canoe or kayak you are skillful in moderate rapids.

*Class IV*—You are an expert who has the proven ability to run difficult rapids in all boats and you are skillful in heavy water and complex rapids.

*Class V*—You are a trip leader with expert boating skills, wide river running experience and good judgment for leading trips on a river.

*Note:* Rafters are by no means ignored by rating systems. Although the above systems were designed primarily for canoeists and kayakers, rafters can rate streams and themselves accordingly. It should be acknowledged that *good* inflatable boats allow for certain mistakes that could prove trouble for canoes and kayaks. However, inflatable boats are better suited for heavy treacherous water, and they are commonly found in waters that might be "suicide" for canoeists and kayakers. The same skill is required for canoeist and rafter alike.

# How to Read the River

**READING A RIVER** means choosing the right course and is probably the most important skill canoeists, kayakers and rafters can develop. The ability to correctly and efficiently read the river's current and character comes from experience. It is the combination of clever reading ability and strong stroking techniques that make good river runners.

Any new stretch of water is first *read* by seeking the information found on *current* printed river guides. Learning the overall character of the river is the most important step in floating. By doing that you will learn *generally* what to expect.

In the *Snake River Guide,* by Verne Huser and Buzz Belknap (Westwater Books), an opening paragraph sets the character of the Snake River as it flows southward from Yellowstone Park.

"River channels change frequently, sometimes overnight. Stumps, overhanging trees, log jams and sand bars may suddenly be laid in or washed away. Inquire locally, secure permits where necessary and inspect your proposed course before undertaking any Snake River trip in your own craft." Later on in the book, describing a particular stretch, "Although there are no rapids in this section, the current is swift and even a small obstruction (a rock or stump) can quickly capsize the inexperienced or careless boatman. Route finding can be a problem. The Snake sends numerous channels braiding their way through the glacial gravels of Jackson Hole (Wyoming); many of these are often blocked by shallow riffles, fallen trees—or even a bull moose."

The character of the Snake River in the vicinity of Jackson Hole is deceptive and ever changing. And it has fooled many people, including myself. Supplemental information can be obtained from the National Park Service, U.S. Forest Service, and Game & Fish Department personnel. Sort the facts from conjecture. Remember, river classifications and difficulty ratings are personal matters. No two rivers are alike. Boating skills vary. Never take a river evaluation as gospel but merely as an aid to support your own skills and knowledge.

Water temperature is a very important consideration to advance river reading information. During spring, summer or fall, for instance, the Snake River runs alarmingly cold. When you pre-read the Snake, you will know not to base your true course entirely on published guides or recommendations. You know the river is basically unpredictable and that few if any mistakes can be made because of the immobilizing water temperature. River charts and topographic maps will help to some extent, but it is your on-river reading skills that will get you through the surprises. Successful river reading depends on keen downstream observation, alertness and pre-trip tips.

## Picking the Right Channel

Some streams have more channels or braids in them than others. Certain stretches of the same river are characteristically open and straight; others, narrow and meandering. It is often the narrow, meandering stretches that are more fun. They present the greater boating challenges.

During high water, most common in the spring, channel selection can be difficult because all waters are running fast. Normal water level obstacles may be covered over, and the wrong channel can be easily taken. Novices or intermediate floaters should consider normal water levels when planning a trip. Float when waters have receded, generally in midsummer or early fall. At normal levels, the best channel to take, provided there are no obstacles, is the deepest, fastest waterway. Faster water commonly washes obstructions away and does not allow a bottom build-up of debris. Successfully and safely running the fastest channel depends on good strokes and a reflex skill of how and when to use them. Skill comes with practice.

## A Slip of the Tongue

River running is full of variables, but a common rule of thumb is to always follow the *tongue* of water. It has a smooth, glistening flow to it, because water is funneled from slow flat water to a fast current at the head of a chute or drop. Follow the tongue because of the unlikelihood of obstacles in the funnel. At the bottom of

1. Here's a downstream ledge. Could be tricky; however, major current flow on right indicates passable spot and tongue.

2. Viewed from above, this ledge looks impassable, and for some it would be best to get out and portage or line the boat. However, where current is strongest and water whitest, a tongue would allow safe passage of canoe or inflatable.

3. In center background is a side eddy. Opposing currents separate the eddy from current and slipping in and out of the eddy can be tricky in canoe or kayak. Note hump of rock to the left and resultant haystack.

4. View upstream shows ledge to the right which would be poor course choice; while slick at left is more favorable. Best course might be right in the middle of the drop, as there are rocks indicated to extreme left of passage.

5. Impossible course? No. Experienced canoeist or kayaker, using full choice of strokes and techniques, could work his way through top center tongue; turn right (going downstream) and drop over chute.

6. Long chute or slick, near rock, is best passage. However, note presence of rocks by churning white water at left. Ledge at right, however, is too risky. Boiling water indicates severe drop.

7. An overall view of above chute or slick (photo #6). Passage near boulder, of course, would be safest.

8. An obvious rock hump and churning white water. Hump is very prominent, not smooth or molded. That means rock is very near the surface and there's a good chance here of snagging or capsizing if rock is hit. Either side of the rock provides safe passage.

Get into good position ahead of time for such obstacles as bridge abutments. Current here could suck the boat into bridge. Amazingly enough, bridge abutments cause a large share of accidents.

the tongue and drop where the gradient flattens, there will be standing waves—the height and force are dependent on the gradient drop, current force, and width of the tongue. Follow the standing waves, as they line out in succession from the chute. You'll get a pretty good ride, but the water is deepest there.

On braided rivers with more than two channel choices, water speed is hard to distinguish. Look for the biggest waves downstream if you can see them. If you can't, take the braid that drops before any of the others. The reason for this is that you can see the drop. Despite the fact it may be shallow, you have "a bird in hand." Those that you cannot see could be obstructed downstream.

### How to Spot Rocks

Some rocks are very obvious; parts of them can be seen above the water. Amazing as it seems, there are a significant number of boaters each season that run into exposed rocks. Negligent downstream observation is usually the cause. Sometimes strokes and techniques are begun too late to steer clear of the obstacle.

Submerged rocks, on the other hand, cause more problems because they are not as obvious and usually feature standing waves immediately downstream of their position. Novices, seeing the waves, do not realize that the upstream rock is the obstacle causing the wave. Sometimes a maneuver is not made in time.

A hump in the water, difficult to see under certain lighting conditions and in choppy water, usually indicates the presence of a rock. There will be times when the hump will not be sighted until you are almost upon it. A quick draw stroke must be taken. Often the hump is spotted with plenty of time to spare. Plan a right or left course around the obstacle instead of waiting until the last few seconds. Where an obvious hump is sighted, there are likely to be others. Scrutinize the water for other possible rocks. Downstream observation and planning is a matter of careful concentration, taking nothing for granted.

Flow patterns over rocks vary with water depth. Shallow water depth over a rock is indicated by a foaming, spitting eddy. As the depth increases over rocks, there is more of a haystack pattern. The latter may not be the best route, but it is ordinarily forgivable; while the former does its best to grab and dump you.

### Fallen Trees Can Be Your Worst Enemies

My wife and I tangled with a beaver-chewed tree at "Spruce's Ditch" in the Snake River one cold day and have never forgotten the incident. Rocks can be forgiving. Fallen trees, with current flowing into them, usually are not. They are traps that can dump, maim and kill. Stretches with downed trees should be carefully read and negotiated. There are times when it might be best to avoid them altogether and portage.

Despite the fact that river rangers commonly patrol popular float stretches looking for dangerous obstacles, fallen trees can occur overnight. High winds, rotted trees, and beavers can change the difficulty rating of a

Above — River channels can change every day. Beaver felled trees can make a safe channel a hazardous one. Right — Water fluctuation from dams is important in understanding the river.

stretch in a mere instant. An "easy" rapid can be changed to an impossible one when a tree falls across the channel.

Take it for granted that when a downed tree is spotted ahead, the current will take you into it unless you take the appropriate actions. Begin maneuvers well ahead of the obstacle by gaining good upstream position so that strokes can be used to avoid it; sticking to the middle or inside bend of the river; or getting out and looking the situation over. In a strong current, a middle position may not be safe enough. Stick further to the inside. When the situation looks too risky or impossible, line the canoe downstream or portage it. That's the better choice than ruining the entire trip.

### The Bend of the River

A bend in the river calls for tactics executed well in advance of the turn by heading the bow sharply toward the inside of the bend while paddling forward. This can be easily accomplished when the bend is sighted in plenty of time. Backpaddling techniques can also be used, holding the stern to the inside bend (setting) and backpaddling around the bend. This is the favored technique when a sharp bend appears suddenly. Back-paddling strokes should be strong and smooth. This is a tough maneuver for beginners to master because proximity to the mouth of the bend can be an unnerving feeling unless paddlers have confidence in their strokes and boat.

### Bridge Abutments

Although rarely talked about, bridge abutments are dangerous. Bridges often signal put-in and take-out points of a river cruise. When boaters put-in slightly upstream of a bridge, they may not have the maneuver-ing time to get into good position to miss the supporting pillars anchored in the water. At the end of the float, weariness and carelessness near the take-out point can account for colliding with abutments.

Abutments are deceivingly treacherous water obstacles, especially if there are several of them stretching across the stream. In swift water, they produce peculiar currents, and the boat not positioned carefully between the pillars could be in for trouble. Abutments also catch logs and debris during high water, and a boater may not have much room to pass through. Bridges located just downstream of sharp bends in the river can produce problems if paddlers are not aware of them. Upstream positioning is important for middle-of-the-abutment passage.

### Low Bridges and Fences

Some streams have an abundance of low water bridges. Fortunately fences are not common. A low water bridge will commonly allow passage of a canoe, raft or kayak to float under it, but that's all. In order to spot such bridges or barbed wire fences, downstream observation is vital. The boat can be beached upstream and lined underneath the obstacle or portaged if that is more practical. Attempting to remain inside a canoe while floating under a low bridge can be extremely dangerous.

### Take-Out Points

It is easy to miss a take-out point unless it is identified by landmarks or signs. Begin take-out maneuvers (paddle rudder or back rowing) well in advance and try to beach the boat in still water or back eddies rather than in swift currents. Remember to hold onto the boat after getting out.

# Reliable Contacts

**THE RIVER** is a fickle lady—moody, mad, low, high, clear, confused, gentle, rough, fast and slow. Her faces are constantly changing. If there is anything at all predictable about her flowing, silver currents, it is the fact that none of them retain any degree of stability for any length of time. A delicately changeable nymph, lady river is subject to even the faintest whims of nature.

Because the spirit is basically unharnessed and the moods and faces change, the river has been a challenge to those who saddle her back with a bucking boat. Whereas winds and storms may temporarily whip the souls of lakes and oceans into frenzied bulls, rivers do not depend on scoldings from nature for their orneriness. They come by that trait naturally. Born in the mountains, with blood current in their veins and a madness to keep moving, rivers are free to create their own mischief by the sheer devilishness of their temperaments. Add to their sinewy strength the wrath of rain and snow runoff, the fall of the terrain, the burden of

heavy squalls, the thirst of droughts, the purity of gin or the milky flow of stale coffee, and the rivers take on their true color—fickle.

Telephone communication can be the floater's best planning tool. It is used to obtain last minute information on water flow, stream levels and weather conditions. A phone call the day before a trip can nearly insure a reliable forecast of what the stream will look like at launch time. If the forecast looks good, plans are activated. When conditions are unfavorable, it might be best to delay the float until they improve.

Letter writing definitely has a place in pre-trip planning. Maps, river charts, access points, camping areas, fishing tips, regulations and stream characteristics can be collected through the mail. Deciding where and when to float can be accomplished at home before vacation time or weekends. A bundle of general information, the groundwork of enjoyable floats, can be researched during winter months. Then that informa-

Reliable contacts make good boating and comfortable camping possible.

Before-the-trip contacts provide valuable information such as maps of the area to be floated.

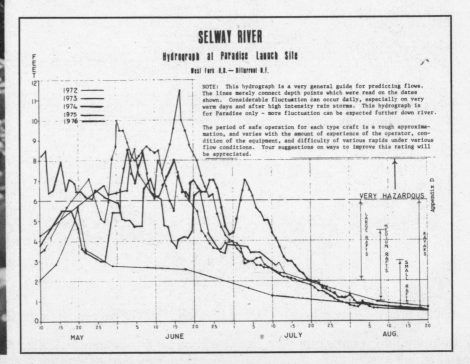

Above—Ordinarily, the more pre-trip planning, the better the float experience. Below—Management agencies can provide information on the best times to float.

SELWAY RIVER
Hydrograph at Paradise Launch Site
West Fork R.D. — Bitterroot N.F.

NOTE: This hydrograph is a very general guide for predicting flows. The lines merely connect depth points which were read on the dates shown. Considerable fluctuation can occur daily, especially on very warm days and after high intensity rain storms. This hydrograph is for Paradise only - more fluctuation can be expected further down river.

The period of safe operation for each type craft is a rough approximation, and varies with the amount of experience of the operator, condition of the equipment, and difficulty of various rapids under various flow conditions. Your suggestions on ways to improve this rating will be appreciated.

tion can be bolstered by current phone queries to learn about variable river conditions.

Governmental agencies that administer public lands, streams and the fish within them are often excellent sources of advance letter and phone contacts. However, boaters should realize that these agencies receive large quantities of correspondence. Requests are often handled by standard printed matter. Most of the information is factual and relatively current, but may not answer specific questions. Therefore, rely on those agencies for basic information and then develop more personal contact sources for detailed information.

Agencies like the U.S. Forest Service (Washington, D.C. 20250), National Park Service (Interior Building, Washington, D.C. 20240), Bureau of Reclamation (Washington, D.C. 20240), Bureau of Land Management (Washington, D.C. 20240), Bureau of Outdoor Recreation (Washington, D.C. 20240), and the U.S. Fish and Wildlife Service (Washington, D.C. 20240) and their regional and state offices can offer good, general information, including listings of floatable rivers along with corresponding maps.

A boater determines beforehand, by consulting state recreation maps, who owns the land and the access to various stretches of river. With this in mind, the appropriate land agencies are contacted. As is often the case with prime, river bottomland, access for floating may be privately controlled. It is up to the boater to secure access permission. Often the agency that can help in pinpointing access is the state fish and game department through local game wardens and fishery personnel.

State fish and game departments are located in the capital city of each state. The main function of these agencies is to maintain and protect the state's fish and wildlife resources. Because of their close working relationship with the outdoors, wardens—the men at the grass roots level—are often the most familiar with floating conditions.

Contact fish and game departments by letter. Your letter may be forwarded to a local warden or information specialist. Or it may be sent back to you with general information and suggestions for making personal contact with an employee in your float area. Either way, local fish and game technicians can be helpful information sources. Quite often they are ardent outdoorsmen in their own right. They are aware of the floating potential of the various waters in their areas. And they can set floaters straight on public and private river access.

It is important to contact these persons in advance of the trip. As their jobs dictate, they spend a good deal of time in the field and are hard to reach at the office or at home. In an off-season letter, during winter or early spring, ask about: 1. good, floatable stretches in their area; 2. public and private access; 3. float difficulty rating; 4. length and average time of float; and 5. fishing or other tips. These questions will yield a wealth of reliable information that can be used later. If you are satisfied with the response you receive and your correspondent appears interested in helping you, request a phone number where he or she may be reached for short notice information.

State parks often provide some of the finest floating potential available. Under the auspices of state fish and game programs and outdoor recreation departments, state parks are meccas for floaters. Pertinent information about state park recreation may be obtained from fish and game departments or recreation offices at the park or state capital headquarters.

Floaters fortunate enough to have friends or relatives living near the local float scene have, perhaps, the best sources of current information.

Good, local float sources outside the governmental agency realm can also be developed. Ordinarily though, these sources produce only after a floater has visited an area once or twice and has developed some personal contacts. Possibly a motel owner or a favorite early morning restaurant cook can be the source of information.

A well-planned trip will include full information on both camping and launching facilities along with up-to-date stream conditions.

# Logistics

FOR THE modern floater, landings are of great significance. Because so much prime river valley land is privately controlled, the floater, for the most part, now depends on public access points administered by the state or federal government.

There was a time when river access through private lands was fairly common and permission relatively easy to obtain. But growing recreational pressure in the last 20 years has changed that situation. There are still some areas where private access is good. But now floaters must rely heavily on land set aside by state fish and game departments, the National Park Service, U.S. Forest Service and Bureau of Reclamation. Since boaters cannot put in or take out just anywhere, the planning of a float trip must include access considerations to and from various stretches of stream.

How does a floater find out where public landings are located? Through the state and federal agencies that administer the land. The agency may own all the land along a significant stretch of river. In that case, reaching landings presents no problems. However, more often than not, public access areas are merely easements that have been obtained specifically for the purpose of public access. The lands along the river may be

Public landings along valuable river frontage are vitally important to every floater — canoeist, kayaker or rafter. Note pickup vehicle that will be left at take-out spot.

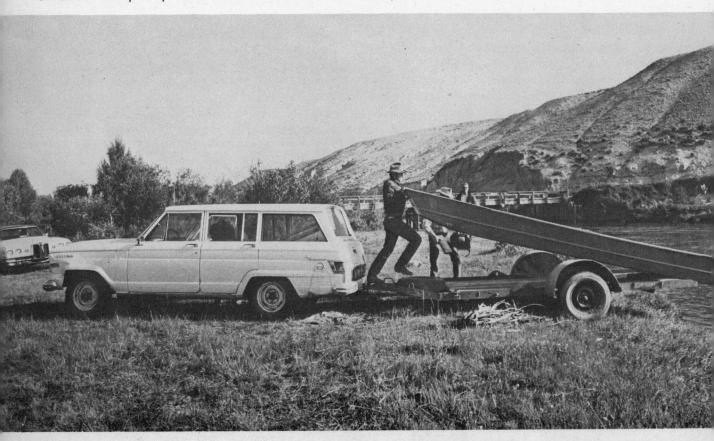

privately owned and public access denied. This is sometimes the case even in the wide open expanses of western states.

Because some waters and the lands that border them are tightly regulated, a floater has the obligation not to violate trespass laws. In other words, fishermen who might innocently beach their boats to fish from shore or fix lunch might be trespassing. And camping is usually out of the question.

To avoid the problems associated with trespassing, the floater has the responsibility to organize floats so landing points or overnight camps are located at public access areas.

When gauging float time, take into account the float craft used, the average speed of the stretch, the time allowed for stops, wind conditions, and time allotted for water obstacles or portages.

### Vehicle Pickups—Rides

One of the considerations you make as a floater is arranging for transportation before you set your boat in the water. There are several alternatives. For two-car families, one of the vehicles can be left at the take-out point. Ideally the pickup vehicle should have the capability of transporting the boat. When using inflatables, the boat can be deflated and stowed in a minimum of space. A cartop boat rack easily handles canoes and

Above—Along some stretches of river even the bicycle can be used for float transportation.

Below—Motorized bike is one means of transportation; it can be chained to a tree at take-out point.

Some resort areas that cater to floaters have pick-up shuttle services between float points.

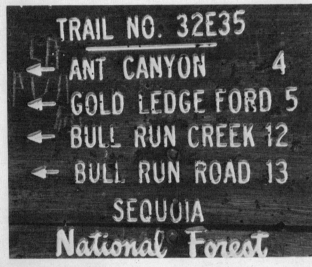

TRAIL NO. 32E35
← ANT CANYON        4
← GOLD LEDGE FORD 5
← BULL RUN CREEK 12
← BULL RUN ROAD 13
SEQUOIA
National Forest

Left—Access points along float stretches are important to floaters planning trips. Maps and signs help indicate distances between points. Below, left —One way to solve logistics problem—a canoe tied to plane's pontoon.

johnboats under 15 feet even on compact cars.

The same type of pickup arrangement can be made among fishing partners—using two vehicles; driving to the take-out point; leaving one of the vehicles there; and returning with the other to the starting point.

Another practical plan is to arrange for someone to meet you at the landing point at a pre-determined time. There are some disadvantages to this alternative. Choose a pickup driver who is reliable and has the directions straight. Decide on a fair price to pay for the service and pay part before the trip and the rest after pickup. Some river resort areas provide commercially operated shuttle service along float stretches.

Here are some other methods. Depending on the length of the float and the access road along the river, a bicycle can be used as a second means of transportation. The bike can be chained to a tree at the take-out point and used to get back to the vehicle after the float. There are limitations to this arrangement of course, but my wife and I have enjoyed this system on a multitude of short (under 6 miles) floats and find the boating and bicycling combination to be quite an adventure. A hoop rack bolted to the back bumper of our vehicle makes for a convenient bike carrier. While one person pedals back to the vehicle, the other person stays with the boat and equipment.

A slightly more sophisticated pickup method utilizes a small, motorized trail bike that can be transported on a frame carrier outside the vehicle. Chained at the take-out landing before the float, a motorbike provides rapid transportation back to the car and is really not as limited by distance factors as the bicycle method.

Still another alternative that can be used on some stretches of water is the addition of an outboard motor to negotiate upstream currents and get back to the starting point. This technique can be practical on slow, deep rivers.

Hitchhiking is another choice for the floater. A boater has two choices. Unload raft and gear at the starting point and have your partner wait there while you drive the vehicle to the take-out point. Then you hitch a ride back to the starting point.

A final, reasonable choice in some areas where a phone is handy is to call a friend or person who has previously consented to pick you up at the take-out point upon receiving your call.

Firm transportation arrangements after the float add to the enjoyment and peace of mind during the trip.

Enjoyment and peace of mind during a float trip are greater when transportation and pickups are arranged before the float rather than left to the end of the trip.

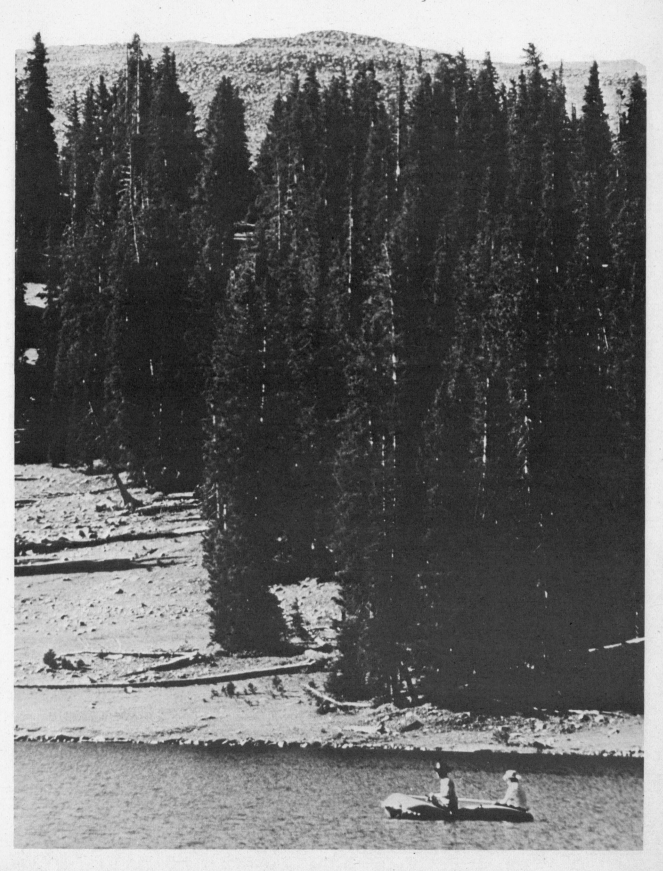

# River Charts and Guides

River charts and guides help canoeists through new and difficult stretches of water.

RECREATIONAL boating maps are distributed by various private and governmental agencies and published by state game and fish departments. They are accurate enough to insure floaters reliable information with enough detail to pre-plan river trips. However, they are not so complicated as to require a navigation course.

Float stretches, located upstream and downstream in fairly close proximity to dams, are usually controlled by the Army Corps of Engineers (Office of the Chief of Engineers, Forrestal Building, Washington, D.C. 20314). The Civil Works Branch, more specifically, and the office of the Fish and Wildlife Section can, at times, help floaters with reliable maps and information. Division offices are located in Vicksburg, Mississippi; Omaha, Nebraska; Waltham, Maine; New York City, New York; Chicago, Illinois; Portland, Oregon; Cincinnati, Ohio; Honolulu, Hawaii; Atlanta, Georgia; San Francisco, California; and Dallas, Texas. Division offices can be contacted by letter for information and contacts at the *district* level of the Corps of Engineers where specific information can be obtained.

The Bureau of Reclamation makes river charts available for some waters. District offices are located at Boise, Idaho; Sacramento, California; Boulder City, Nevada; Salt Lake City, Utah; Amarillo, Texas; Billings, Montana; and Denver, Colorado.

The U.S. Geological Survey (National Center, Reston, Virginia 22092) is a research agency under the Interior Department. This agency maps the nation's physical features, including water resources and can be the best source of accurate maps for the floater. The Map Information Office (U.S. Geological Survey, Washington, D.C. 20242) is the place to write for general mapping information. For float areas east of the Mississippi, write to Distribution Section, Geological Survey, Washington, D.C. 20242. Waters and lands west of the Mississippi are handled by the Distribution Center, Geological Survey, Denver Federal Center, Denver, Colorado 80225.

Maps can also be obtained from the Bureau of Outdoor Recreation in Washington, D.C., and from national, district and local headquarters of the National Park Service and U.S. Forest Service that govern waters flowing within their boundaries.

In some areas, the Coast Guard (400 7th St., S.W., Washington, D.C. 20590) can play a role in disseminat-

U.S. Forest Service maps show river stretches,
access points and general terrain features.

Above—Topographic map that shows land and water contours and elevations. An excellent source for planning trips in relatively unknown areas, it can also be used to find best portage routes. Below—Example of topographic map symbols used in river running.

## TOPOGRAPHIC MAP SYMBOLS
### VARIATIONS WILL BE FOUND ON OLDER MAPS

| | |
|---|---|
| Hard surface, heavy duty road, four or more lanes | Boundary, national |
| Hard surface, heavy duty road, two or three lanes | State |
| Hard surface, medium duty road, four or more lanes | County, parish, municipio |
| Hard surface, medium duty road, two or three lanes | Civil township, precinct, town, barrio |
| Improved light duty road | Incorporated city, village, town, hamlet |
| Unimproved dirt road and trail | Reservation, national or state |
| Dual highway, dividing strip 25 feet or less | Small park, cemetery, airport, etc. |
| Dual highway, dividing strip exceeding 25 feet | Land grant |
| Road under construction | Township or range line, United States land survey |
| | Township or range line, approximate location |
| Railroad, single track and multiple track | Section line, United States land survey |
| Railroads in juxtaposition | Section line, approximate location |
| Narrow gage, single track and multiple track | Township line, not United States land survey |
| Railroad in street and carline | Section line, not United States land survey |
| Bridge, road and railroad | Section corner, found and indicated |
| Drawbridge, road and railroad | Boundary monument; land grant and other |
| Footbridge | United States mineral or location monument |
| Tunnel, road and railroad | |
| Overpass and underpass | Index contour / Intermediate contour |
| Important small masonry or earth dam | Supplementary contour / Depression contours |
| Dam with lock | Fill / Cut |
| Dam with road | Levee / Levee with road |
| Canal with lock | Mine dump / Wash |
| | Tailings / Tailings pond |
| Buildings (dwelling, place of employment, etc.) | Strip mine / Distorted surface |
| School, church, and cemetery | Sand area / Gravel beach |
| Buildings (barn, warehouse, etc.) | |
| Power transmission line | Perennial streams / Intermittent streams |
| Telephone line, pipeline, etc. (labeled as to type) | Elevated aqueduct / Aqueduct tunnel |
| Wells other than water (labeled as to type) | Water well and spring / Disappearing stream |
| Tanks; oil, water, etc. (labeled as to type) | Small rapids / Small falls |
| Located or landmark object; windmill | Large rapids / Large falls |
| Open pit, mine, or quarry; prospect | Intermittent lake / Dry lake |
| Shaft and tunnel entrance | Foreshore flat / Rock or coral reef |
| | Sounding, depth curve / Piling or dolphin |
| | Exposed wreck / Sunken wreck |
| Horizontal and vertical control station: | Rock, bare or awash; dangerous to navigation |
|   Tablet, spirit level elevation | |
|   Other recoverable mark, spirit level elevation | Marsh (swamp) / Submerged marsh |
| Horizontal control station; tablet, vertical angle elevation | Wooded marsh / Mangrove |
|   Any recoverable mark, vertical angle or checked elevation | Woods or brushwood / Orchard |
| Vertical control station; tablet, spirit level elevation | Vineyard / Scrub |
|   Other recoverable mark, spirit level elevation | Inundation area / Urban area |
| Checked spot elevation | |
| Unchecked spot elevation and water elevation | |

ing information to the general public. Most often, regional Notice to Mariners and Marine Aids to Navigation are available for those waterways that share commercial and recreational boating uses. The locations of district offices can be obtained by writing to the main headquarters in Washington, D.C. Floaters can then contact regional or local branches of the Coast Guard for current, specific information about particular sections of rivers under Coast Guard jurisdiction.

Another source for maps are various Chambers of Commerce, located in towns near popular float streams. Chamber maps can offer good information. However, most of them are in need of weeding out facts from advertising come-ons.

Privately published river guides and maps are often sold in recreation areas and towns near popular stretches of river. When updated regularly, these guides can be accurate and helpful. However, be sure to look for the copyright date in the guide or on the maps. For swift, changeable western rivers especially, charts older than 3 years might be outdated to the point that they can do more harm than good. Because there is usually some desire for financial return in the commercial production of river guides or maps, a number of charts are not kept current enough to insure their reliability. It is a good idea not to depend on one guide or map as the final word for trip planning. A combination of commercially sold float guides and state or federal maps can prove valuable in double checking information and accuracy. The more time spent with several good maps of the float stretch, the more peace of mind can be enjoyed during the trip.

What should a good float chart or guide contain? In general a good float map should be broken down into various stretches. Charts should be detailed enough to illustrate all essential float information in clear, easy-to-read form. Guides containing several maps and bound in a small book or loose-leaf form are more handy. Each section of floatable water should be broken down into miles. The best charts show distances between easily recognizable man-made or natural landmarks such as bridges, dikes, rapids, feeder streams, dramatic bends in the river, signs or campgrounds. By knowing the number of miles traveled the floater can determine whether the pace should be quickened to reach the final destination at the specific time.

Topographic maps, available from the U.S. Geological Survey, give an accurate picture of a river. Distances can be measured fairly accurately by the natural and man-made features symbolized on the "topo."

River charts should show, through various signs and symbols clearly printed on the map, the location of dikes, levees or falls. Rapids of any significance are

A good river guide will indicate what stretches are suited for beginners.

Even canoe races require foreknowledge of river conditions through the use of proper maps and guides.

usually represented by solid bars on the map overlaying the stream. The more prominent features that are indicated on a map, the better a floater can determine distance covered. Picnic areas and campgrounds are shown on some maps. Creeks entering the main stream are named. Trails and portages are well defined. Obvious hills, mountain peaks, bluffs and meadows are indicated. Bridges that cross the stream or roads that parallel its course are marked. Ranches or farmsteads that can be viewed from the river are listed. Public landings, of course, are well defined.

Some maps go beyond normal information, listing such highlights as best fishing spots, historic points of interest, and gravel bars. Streams of rare, year-round stability are sometimes defined by in-stream boulders, fallen logs, riffle areas or common trouble spots. These excellent beginner streams are in the minority though. Most rivers because of their fluctuating water levels are not defined by their in-stream watermarks for obvious reasons, and ordinarily only the most prominent of trouble spots are indicated.

Some maps have some helpful notations like "difficult turn in high water" or "log obstacle during low water" or "tricky rapids with rocks all year." These "extras" are fine for some stretches and some streams. However, water safety experts have discovered that some boaters rely too heavily on charts that pinpoint trouble spots. They tend to let their guards down and often run into unexpected snags or rocks.

Some river guides also go into brief descriptions of the river and then evaluate each stretch. This gives the beginning floater or newcomer to the river an overall idea of what to expect. It's smart to keep in mind, though, that most recreational charts are merely aids. They can help the floater immensely. But their accuracy, dictated by the moods of the river, cannot compare, let's say, to the always predictable road map that seldom changes. In addition to good charts and guides then, a floater must combine boating skills and sound, common sense.

# Your Legal Right to Float

"As long ago as the Institutes of Justinian, running waters, like the air and the sea, were things common to all and property of none." *(United States* v. *Gerlach Live Stock Co.)*

And then man discovered the power of water control.

The Massachusetts Bay Colony Ordinance of 1641-7 provides:

"Sec. 2. Every inhabitant who is a householder shall have free fishing and fowling in any great ponds, bays, coves and rivers, so far as the sea ebbs and flows within the precincts of the town where they dwell, unless the freemen of the said town, or the general court, have otherwise appropriated them . . .

"Sec. 4. And for great ponds lying in common, though within the bounds of some town, it shall be free for any man to fish or fowl there, and may pass and repass on foot through any man's propriety for that end, so they trespass not upon any man's corner meadow."

There have been, even in the earliest days, laws to help define public waters and access to them. In the course of time, the laws, naturally, have become more complex and harder to define with a multitude of different meanings. To say that one needs a lawyer to decode modern day water laws, as they pertain to river floaters, would be a gross understatement. It is nearly impossible for the layman to obtain a clear understanding of his water rights without the help of an attorney.

I have personally passed up some fine looking float water because I was unsure of its status. But, knowledgeable floaters can gain a command of how to interpret water laws or where to go for clarification. Research can prevent the floater from being "bluffed out" of a float trip by the harsh words of a landowner or intimidated by warning or trespass signs that could be illegal.

An attorney is a reliable source of information about water laws. I contacted my good friend, Timothy J. Bommer, an attorney of excellent reputation as well as an ardent outdoorsman from Jackson Hole, Wyoming. Bommer lives in the heart of floating country, with the Snake, Green, Henry's Fork and New Fork Rivers

Even in vast lands of the West, access is becoming difficult.

nearly at his doorstep. Tim displayed a sincere and enthusiastic interest in my query about legal floating rights, forewarning me, "The question you ask involves a complex area of the law."

### Why All the Confusion?

According to Bommer, most laymen assume that all "navigable" waters of the country can be legally floated by the public. "The word, 'navigable,' is not a clearly defined word," said Bommer, "and herein lies a reason for the confusion. All surface water throughout the United States is generally subject either to federal or state jurisdiction. There continues to be a raging controversy between the United States and state governments as to the ownership of water in the states."

In other words, states define their navigable waters one way, and the federal government may define them another. Bommer poses a question, "Should the Green River (a magnificent, blue-ribbon trout and floating stream in Wyoming) be impounded at three locations to provide hydroelectric energy for Los Angeles? If the Green were determined navigable, or affected navigable waters controlled by the United States, the federal government could then make the decision of what would happen to Wyoming's water and build three dams on the Green River. But on the other hand, should the state of Wyoming be allowed to determine that more benefit would be derived through recreation and agricultural uses? It's complicated."

A few points to remember: 1. The most highly developed body of federal water law is in relation to navigable waters. 2. Since the national powers are supreme, the United States government's action in reference to a navigable river is not subject to state laws which, on the surface, seem to apply to all waters. 3. In *Arizona* v. *California*, the Supreme Court declared that the power to dam and store the water of a navigable stream gives the power to distribute the water to states in such shares as Congress or its delegate may determine.

That's a brief overview of the federal/state water law problem. Now down to state level.

### Where Does Your State Stand?

Navigable waters of the various states are defined by the states themselves. Some states have apparently made no attempt to create a definition of "navigability" or "public waters." These states are: Arizona, Arkansas, Colorado, Connecticut, Delaware, Florida, Hawaii, Kansas, Kentucky, Maine, Maryland, Nebraska, Nevada, New Jersey, North Carolina, Pennsylvania, Rhode Island, Tennessee, Washington, and West Virginia.

Court decisions in Missouri, New Mexico, Wisconsin, and Wyoming have placed varying degrees of emphasis on state constitutional declarations when establishing a broad foundation for recreational surface uses. New Mexico and Wyoming appear to have taken the strongest position on this point. The New Mexico Constitution states: "The unappropriated water of every natural stream is hereby declared to belong to the public."

The Wyoming Constitution provides that the water of the state belongs to the state and therefore belongs to the public. In the rather unique *Day* v. *Armstrong* case, the decision holds that even if a particular stream is "nonnavigable" the water flowing through that stream is a public easement, and can therefore be used by the

Some states declare that the shoreline is public. . . .

public. The decision went one step further in allowing the public to reasonable trespass across private lands in the event of an obstruction in the water course.

The Wyoming Constitution further states, "Persons and their property may only float by boat, canoe or raft for any lawful purpose down that part of any stream in the State of Wyoming where the records of the state engineer for the ten years preceding such floating show that part of the stream to have had an average flow of water for the month of July exceeding 1,000 cubic feet per second."

The Wisconsin Constitution provides, "The River Mississippi and the navigable waters leading into the Mississippi and St. Lawrence, and the carrying places between the same, shall be common highways and forever free, as well to the inhabitants of the state as to the citizens of the United States, without any tax, impost or duty therefore."

The Texas definition reads this way. "All streams so far as they retain an average width of thirty feet from the mouth up shall be considered navigable streams."

California and Illinois represent the legislative patterns in which navigable waters are defined in a commercial context, essentially limited to transportation uses.

Historical overtones permeate the Mississippi provision. "All rivers, creeks, and bayous in this state, twenty-five miles in length, that have sufficient depth and width of water for thirty consecutive days in the year, for floating a steamboat with carrying capacity of two hundred bales of cotton, are hereby declared to be navigable waters of this state."

A product of the Land and Water Law Review of 1971 is a passage drafted which is an attempt to codify the common law concerning rights in public waters—a nearly impossible task. It reads, "A river, stream, creek or channel which, during any stage, including the ordinary high water stages, has been or is being used or is capable of being used in its natural and ordinary condition for floating any boat, canoe, skiff or craft with at least one person aboard, or for floating products for transportation purposes, is declared public."

### Floaters Can Find Answers

You can see, by the various examples of water laws, why some landowners have gotten away with illegal obstacles to "navigable" or public waters. Confusion and lack of definition have been on their side. As recreational river use increases, more attempts to close or block certain waters are being made. It is important for you, the floater, to know the laws in your state. And it is wise, even to the point of sounding ridiculous, to carry a copy of those laws with you when floating. You can take steps beforehand to insure that your public water rights are not violated or threatened.

1. At least one month before your trip, write to the Attorney General of the state in which you live or wish to float for the laws pertaining to the ownership and use of the water within that state. Carry a copy of these laws with you when you float.

2. Check with your local fish and game department to determine what waters can and cannot be used by the public in accordance with the laws of the state.

3. No matter what the law states, always make inquiries as to the floatability of unfamiliar waters. Some landowners can be hostile, regardless of the law. Certain stretches can be dangerously blocked. A few floats may not be worth the battle.

. . . .other states have trespass laws that prohibit even a hand from contact.

# Wild and Scenic Rivers

**EVERY FLOATER** should cultivate a sincere and unyielding interest in the *National Wild And Scenic Rivers System*. It is by far the most important law affecting streams, rivers, lands and the people who love them. Authorized by the Wild and Scenic Rivers Act (Public Law 90-542) on October 2, 1968, and amended by Congress (Public Law 93-621) to include 29 additional rivers for study, the System is a product of beauty. Despite its vulnerability to politics and big money, the System lives and works. A remarkable tribute (in a time of relentless energy demands, commercial water hoarding and inflated land prices) to the men and women who fought to preserve the water roots of America.

## The National Wild and Scenic Rivers System

The Wild and Scenic Rivers Act declares: " . . . Certain selected rivers of the Nation which, with their immediate environments, possess outstandingly remarkable scenic, recreational, geologic, fish and wildlife, historic, cultural or other similar values, shall be preserved in free-flowing condition, and that they and their immediate environments shall be protected for the benefit and enjoyment of present and future generations. The Congress declares that the established national policy of dam and other construction at appropriate sections of the rivers of the United States needs to be complemented by a policy that would preserve other selected rivers or sections thereof in their free-flowing condition to protect the water quality of such rivers and to fulfill other vital national conservation purposes."

## How the System Was Implemented

Congress established the National Wild and Scenic Rivers System and designated all or portions of eight rivers as the initial components of that system to be administered by the Department of the Interior or the Department of Agriculture. Those rivers designated were the Rio Grande (New Mexico), Saint Croix, Wolf, Eleven Point, Middle Fork of the Feather, Middle Fork of the Clearwater, Middle Fork of the Salmon and the Rogue.

The 1968 Act designated 27 other rivers for detailed study as potential additions to the National System. On January 3, 1975, the Congress amended the Act, adding 29 rivers for study. In addition to the original eight rivers, the Snake (Idaho), Rapid, Lower St. Croix, Chattooga and New River are now included in the System and administered by the federal government. The Little Beaver, Little Miami and Allagash, also part of the System, are currently being administered on a state or local basis, but also have federal protection. Under certain conditions, the Secretary of the Interior can add a select state or locally administered river area to the National Wild Scenic Rivers System upon application of the governor.

## Criteria for Inclusion

All rivers in the National System must be substantially free-flowing and have water of high quality or water that could be restored to that condition. The river and adjacent lands must also be in a natural or esthetically pleasing condition and possess outstanding scenic, recreational, geologic, fish and wildlife, historic, cultural or other similar values.

Because all rivers are different and some have been altered in varying degrees, there are three classifications for inclusion in the National Wild and Scenic Rivers System. These are Wild River Areas, Scenic River Areas and Recreational River Areas. Basically, the Wild River Area is the most primitive, inaccessible and unchanged. It is managed to preserve and enhance the primitive qualities. A Scenic River Area can be accessible in places by road and is managed to preserve and enhance a natural, though sometimes modified, environment and provide a modest range of facilities for recreation. Recreational River Areas may have undergone some development and impoundment or diversion in the past. They are managed to provide the visitor with a wide range of readily accessible recreational opportunities which may reflect evidence of man's activity, yet remain esthetically pleasing.

Because of the wisdom of people who were willing to fight for and defend free-flowing rivers in the United States, canoeists, rafters and kayakers will benefit. Not

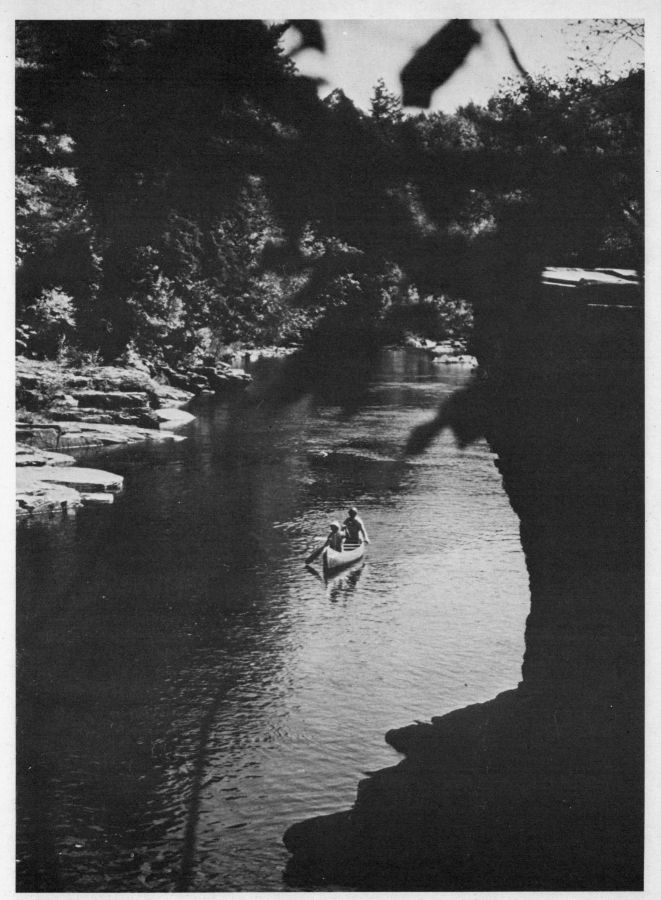

Because of concerned persons and wise legislation, some rivers and streams will be kept free and unchanged.

Some rivers are not protected by Wild and Scenic River regulations—the results are self-evident.

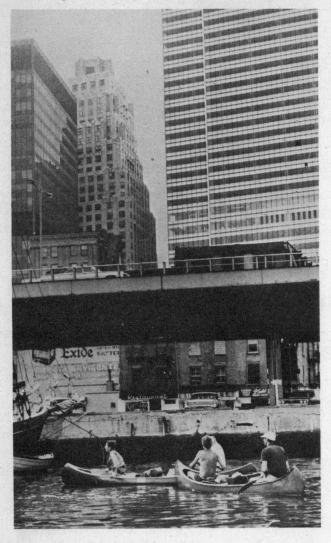

only will we enjoy a variety of streams in their natural or semi-natural state, but so will our children and their children. However, the fight is far from over. Complacency threatens progress already made and deters the inclusion of other qualified rivers into the System.

The Wild and Scenic Rivers Act does not prohibit the construction of roads or bridges, timber harvesting and livestock grazing or "other uses that do not *substantially* interfere with full public use and enjoyment." Mining and related mineral activities must be conducted in accord with the provisions of the Wild and Scenic Rivers Act.

While these activities may not be disastrous in themselves, past performance demonstrates the need for caution. Unnecessary road building, timber sales allocated to unscrupulous clear cutters, overgrazing and strip mining all affect existing Wild and Scenic Rivers and can block the inclusion of rivers under consideration.

Any floater who feels protective about the stream that affords so much floating, fishing, camping, nature, or photographic pleasure can contribute, in some way, to monitoring and safeguarding her wild and scenic virtues. We can support legislation aimed at adding more rivers to the System.

For our efforts, we are richly rewarded. The privilege of public access to waters and lands of remarkable beauty and quality is but part of the bounty. Floating a Wild and Scenic River is a personal matter—a special communion between floater and river. It is a testimony: here lies a stream forever saved from the complexities of modern man. Clean water, fish, trees, meandering courses, birds, animals, stillness, canoes, kayaks, and inflatable boats—that's what a Wild and Scenic River is.

## RIVER MILEAGE CLASSIFICATIONS FOR COMPONENTS OF NATIONAL WILD AND SCENIC RIVERS SYSTEM

| River<br>Present Units — National System | Administering<br>Agency | Miles by Classification | | | Total<br>Miles |
|---|---|---|---|---|---|
| | | Wild | Scenic | Recreational | |
| 1. Middle Fork Clearwater, Idaho | USFS | 54 | — | 131 | 185 |
| 2. Eleven Point, Missouri | USFS | — | 44.4 | — | 44.4 |
| 3. Feather, California | USFS | 32.9 | 9.7 | 65.4 | 108 |
| 4. Rio Grande, New Mexico | BLM/USFS | 51.75 | — | 1 | 52.75 |
| | (BLM) | (43.90) | — | (0.25) | (44.15) |
| | (USFS) | (7.85) | — | (0.75) | (8.60) |
| 5. Rogue, Oregon | BLM/USFS | 33 | 7.5 | 44 | 84.5 |
| | (BLM) | (20) | — | (27) | (47) |
| | (USFS) | (13) | (7.5) | (17) | (37.5) |
| 6. St. Croix, Minnesota And Wis. | NPS | — | 181 | 19 | 200 |
| 7. Middle Fork Salmon, Idaho | USFS | 103 | — | 1 | 104 |
| 8. Wolf, Wisconsin | NPS | — | 25 | — | 25 |
| 9. Allagash Wilderness Waterway, Me. | Maine | 95 | — | — | 95 |
| 10. Lower St. Croix, Minn. and Wis. | NPS | — | 12 | 15 | 27 |
| | Minn. & Wis. | — | — | 25 | 25 |
| 11. Chattooga, N.C., S.C., and Ga. | USFS | 39.8 | 2.5 | 14.6 | 56.9 |
| 12. Little Miami, Ohio | Ohio | — | 18 | 48 | 66 |
| 13. Little Beaver, Ohio | Ohio | — | 33 | — | 33 |
| 14. Snake, Idaho and Oregon | USFS | 32.5 | 34.4 | — | 66.9 |
| 15. Rapid, Idaho | USFS | 31 | — | — | 31 |
| 16. New, North Carolina | North Carolina | — | 26.5 | — | 26.5 |
| Total | | 472.95 | 394.0 | 364.0 | 1,230.95 |

## Important Roles for River Lovers

We can take active roles in initiating new legislation or safeguarding the existing Wild and Scenic River System. A most important point to remember is that river lovers, like yourself, are responsible for preserving many of our beautiful streams. Action was no doubt initiated at water level, by common, ordinary citizens who witnessed the pollution of our nation's waterways and were sickened by it.

First of all, thoroughly acquaint yourself with the Wild and Scenic Rivers Act by obtaining a copy from the Department of the Interior, Bureau of Outdoor Recreation, Washington, D.C. 20240; or Department of Agriculture, Forest Service, Washington, D.C. 20250. From either of these two agencies you can obtain a copy of the Act and pamphlets *Wild and Scenic Rivers* and *Guidelines for Evaluating Wild, Scenic, and Recreational Areas* along with a map of current and proposed rivers. Then you will have the facts as they stand.

Under the System, rivers are listed in various categories, such as: existing components of the System; studies completed; and studies in progress. Studies must be completed by law on specified dates. A significant portion of the river candidates have studies still in progress. Here is where your voice and actions can be heard and felt. Investigate the study. Is the time consuming research legitimate and necessary to the total criteria of a certain river or is there lack of interest, political red tape and strong opposition by powerful money interests?

The Wild and Scenic Rivers Act encourages state and local governments to participate in the program. Local and state representatives and senators should be contacted. Remember, there is strength in numbers. Join a canoe club, a sportsmen organization, or a state or national conservation group. Letters, phone calls, petitions and personal visits all work. It is your governor who has the option of applying for inclusion in the national Wild and Scenic Rivers System. When it comes time to vote, find out how your representatives and gubernatorial candidates feel about Wild and Scenic Rivers. Getting the job done involves some politicking.

The Environmental Protection Agency, Corps of Engineers, State Water Pollution Control Agency, State Engineers Office, and Fish and Game Department are offices that wield powers over the future of our float waters. Know their addresses. Write letters when you have questions regarding local or national problems. Attend public hearings. Monitor water pollution with simple water-quality sampling techniques. When we take active roles in guarding the streams we love, and preserving their future, then we realize the full meaning and responsibility of floating a wild and scenic river.

Hard fighting on the part of river lovers preserves streams for future generations.

# Good Reading and Information

**BOOK AND** magazine days are those wintry times not fit for man or canoe. Nestle in front of fire or heater and bask in the adventures of others. If you love river floating and are eager to learn and if you delight in words of advice and relish the adventures of others, prime your mind through reading for that first, delicious day in spring before runoff when you and your boat will make the first trip of the season. There is no perfect book for everybody. And not every author will say what you want to hear. Sift through the good and the mediocre and garner treasures that will make you a better floater and outdoorsman who appreciates what nature has to offer. There is a world of floating adventure in books, magazines and booklets:

### Paddling

*Best Canoe Book Ever* (Davidson and Rugge). First-hand adventure.

*Boatbuilder's Manual* (Walbridge). How to build your own fiberglass canoes and kayaks.

*Canoeing* (Michaelson & Ray). Information on equipment with good instruction.

*Canoeing and Kayaking* (Ruck) All aspects of canoeing and kayaking.

*Canoeing for Children* (Malo).

*Canoeing Wilderness Waters* (Heberton Evans III). Covers the essentials.

*Canoe Poling* (Beletz). Comprehensive study of the subject.

*Guide to Paddle Adventure* (Kemmer). Beginner's manual for paddling.

*Kayaking* (Evans & Anderson). Covers all phases of kayaking—the "bible."

*Pole, Paddle and Portage* (Riviere). How-to book on techniques.

*River Running* (Huser). Comprehensive guide for river running with inflatables.

*Survival of the Bark Canoe* (McPhee). With sketches.

*Whitewater Canoeing* (Sandreuter). Complete white water instruction.

*Wilderness Canoeing* (Malo). A good how-to manual.

### Canoeing and Camping

*Campground Cooking* (Farmer). Good food ideas for boat and trail camping.

*Camper's Digest* (Bauer). Covers every phase of outdoor adventure.

*Canoe Camper's Handbook* (Bearse). Complete outdoor adventure.

*Malo's Complete Guide to Canoeing & Canoe Camping* (Malo).

### Fishing and Photography

*Backpack Fishing* (Farmer). Lightweight, compactable techniques for boat and trail.

*Fishermen's Digest* (Bauer). Everything a fisherman needs to know.

*Hunting With a Camera* (Bauer). How to stalk game with lens from land or boat.

*Outdoor Photographer's Digest* (Bauer). Real adventure in outdoor photography.

*The ABC's of Fishing* (Zwirz). From novice to expert.

*Trout Fishermen's Digest* (Richey). How and where to catch big trout.

### Nature and Wildlife

*Birds of North America* (Robbins, Bruun, Zim & Singer). Good identification book.

*Outdoor Lore* (Ormond). Covers *all* outdoor lore and techniques.

*Reptiles and Amphibians* (Zim, Smith). Easy guide for quick identification.

*Sand County Almanac* (Leopold). Puts nature and environment in perspective.

*Wildlife Illustrated* (Ovington). 240 American game birds, animals and fish.

### Booklets

*Basic Canoeing* (Hasenfus-American Red Cross). The "bible" of canoeing.

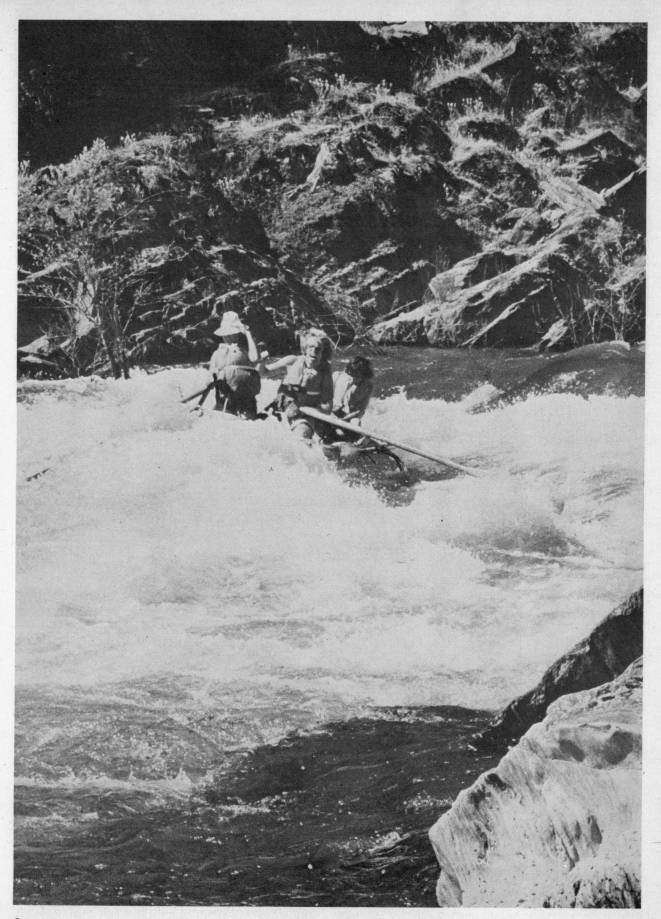

Good books are now available on the techniques of white water rafting.

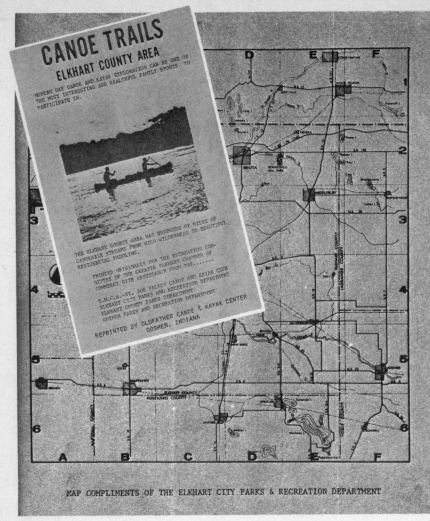

**CANOE TRAILS**
ELKHART COUNTY AREA

MODERN DAY CANOE AND KAYAK EXPLORATION CAN BE ONE OF THE MOST INTERESTING AND HEALTHFUL FAMILY SPORTS TO PARTICIPATE IN.

THE ELKHART COUNTY AREA HAS HUNDREDS OF MILES OF CANOEABLE STREAMS FROM WILD WILDERNESS TO BEAUTIFUL RESIDENTIAL PADDLING.

PRINTED ORIGINALLY FOR THE RECREATION COMMITTEE OF THE GREATER ELKHART CHAMBER OF COMMERCE WITH ASSISTANCE FROM THE......

Y.M.C.A.-ST. JOE VALLEY CANOE AND KAYAK CLUB
ELKHART CITY PARKS AND RECREATION DEPARTMENT
ELKHART COUNTY PARKS DEPARTMENT
GOSHEN PARKS AND RECREATION DEPARTMENT

REPRINTED BY OLDFATHER CANOE & KAYAK CENTER
GOSHEN, INDIANA

MAP COMPLIMENTS OF THE ELKHART CITY PARKS & RECREATION DEPARTMENT

THE ELKHART RIVER - A narrow river tumbling through farmland, much of which is wooded - upstream from the Goshen Pond can be dangerous at high water levels - good campsites - fishing for small mouth bass, pike and redeye. 2 to 6 feet deep on the average.

- Hwy. 13 (So. of Millersburg to Benton at Hwy. 33, 1½ hrs.
- Benton (by river) to Baintertown (east of Hwy. 15, So of Goshen) 3½ hrs.
- Benton (by canal) to Baintertown, 2½ hrs.
- Baintertown to Goshen Pond Dam, 3 hrs.
- Goshen Dam to Rogers Park on north side of Goshen, 1 hr.
- Rogers Park to Oxbow County Park, 2½ hrs.
- Oxbow Park to Studebaker Park in Elkhart, 2½ hrs.
- Studebaker Park to Island Park at the confluence of the Elkhart and St. Joseph Rivers, ½ hr.
- Island Park to McNaughton Park (on the St. Joseph River, 1 hr.

Downstream from McNaughton Park there are quite a few powerboats operating and caution should be observed.

THE ST. JOSEPH RIVER - A beautiful river - wide in some stretches - excellent fishing for small mouth bass, pike and catfish - upstream from Elkhart. Runs through wooded areas where wild animals and birds and an occasional deer can be observed - many blue herons - runs 3 to 6 feet in depth on the average.

- Three Rivers to Constantine Dam, 3½ hrs
- Constantine Dam to Mottville Dam, 2½ hrs.

Each area has its own local float guides and tips booklets. They are very helpful provided they are current.

*Basic Sailing* (American Red Cross). All-around guide applicable for canoe sailing.

*Fundamentals of Kayaking* (Evans). Teaching guide for kayaking.

*Group-Camping by Canoe* (Grumman Boat Co.). The basics of trip logistics.

*Grumman Book Rack* (Grumman Boat Co.). Complete list of books and guides for canoeists.

*Rent-A-Canoe Directory* (Grumman Boat Co.). Canoe rentals coast-to-coast.

*White Water Handbook for Canoe and Kayak* (Urban). Good all-around guide.

### Magazines

*Camping & Backpacking Journals* (Davis Publications). Camping techniques and some floating articles.

*Canoe* (American Canoe Association). Complete canoe, kayak and poling coverage.

*Canoe News* (U.S. Canoe Association). Canoeing news and adventure.

*Down River* (edited by Eric Evans). Covers white water river sport.

*Whitewater Journal* (American Whitewater Affiliation). Whitewater running.

### State and Regional River Guides

Nearly every state in the country that has a significant number of floatable waters within its boundaries produces state or regional guides to floatable waters and best techniques for running them. Some guides are published by the state or county, National Park Service, U.S. Forest Service or Bureau of Outdoor Recreation. Others are published on a commercial basis. A *good* state or regional guide can be the best source of reliable information—provided it is current. You can inquire at libraries and bookstores for locally published information. The combination of accurate, current, local guides and maps and good river skills, add up to happy, safe float trips.

# Basic Boat Knots

CANOEISTS, kayakers and rafters can avoid lost boats, broken fingernails and lost tempers if they learn a few basic knots. Unlike the square knot, the following knots hold boats securely, are easy to tie and loosen and do not jam.

## Bowline

The best knot for making a loop that won't slip or for tying two ropes together. Form a loop in one hand, pass the free end through that loop, around the standing part, then back the loop through, as illustrated.

## Sheet Bend

This knot joins ropes of different sizes and materials. The form of the Sheet Bend is identical to that of the Bowline. Form a loop with one end of a rope. Take the end of another rope through that loop and tuck the end of it under the form where it came through, making sure to cross over both parts of the opposite rope.

## Clove Hitch

A good knot to use for securing bow and stern lines to moorings. Bring the end of the rope over or around the mooring post. Bring the end down, under, and up at the left side of the standing part. Cross the end over the standing part, make another turn down around the post, bringing the end up again, and under its own loop to the right of the standing part of the rope.

1—Basic Hitch

2 — Looped end easy to untie when wet.

Mooring Post

## Lashing Knot

When lashing down cargo packs to the bottom of the boat and to thwarts or for lashing deflated pack rafts to pack frames, various lash knots will do the job. Most important, remember to balance the load first and this can be done by using several smaller pack sacks rather than one big one where weight shift is likely and balance would be difficult. Lashing is basically using the same alternate cross cords as you do when lacing a shoe, beginning with a slip knot starter. Half hitches can be used to retain tension on the lashing and to tighten diagonal rope twists. Finish lashing off with a clove hitch that is easy to untie, even when wet.

## Butterfly Noose

This is a loop knot that won't jam and can be used for hand holds in pulling. Twist a loop and then fold the lower part of the loop and pull it through the center.

1

2

3

Diagonal "shoe lace" lashing on cargo bag.

Clove Hitch loop finish.

# The American Canoe Association

"**DO YOU LOVE** nature—hate noise? Do you prefer to spend leisure time enjoying what's left of our natural environment—in the mountains, forests and deserts, the lakes, rivers and streams? Do you like to camp, hike, swim and ski? Do you love the spirit of competition? The American Canoe Association is in a pretty good position to know what makes a canoe or kayak paddler tick. One nice opportunity you have in store is that the 'not too many' friends you choose share your views about the outdoors. So the canoeist you meet 20 miles up the river is getting away from it, maybe daydreaming a little, like you. A canoeist is often a fast friend, even before you learn his last name. You don't have to own a canoe or kayak to belong to the ACA. All that is necessary is an interest in one or more of the

campaigns on issues that affect the waterways and access to them. As with most environmentally concerned groups, there is strength in numbers. It is through the Association that individuals can make their feelings known as well as take active roles in public hearings concerning river use and development.

The Association is a member of the International Canoe Federation and represents American canoeists in all international canoeing matters. As "Class A" members of the U.S. Olympic Committee, the ACA serves as the sport's governing body for all American canoeists in national and international competition.

One benefit of the ACA that proves helpful to many canoeists is information on river trails, canoe cruises and touring. Members of the ACA can obtain this in-

Organized In 1880

**American Canoe Association**

**National Headquarters:** 4260 EAST EVANS AVENUE, DENVER, COLORADO 80222
Telephone (303) 758-8257

many different recreational or competitive activities of canoe sport."—from *Canoe with the ACA* (The American Canoe Association, organized in 1880.)

Because the sports of canoeing and kayaking are learned better from qualified instructors and enjoyed more by groups of people, the American Canoe Association provides a strong voice for organized canoeists across the country. Whether solitary paddlers or canoe club members, everyone concerned about the two sports and the preservation and protection of fine canoeing and kayaking waterways benefits from the ACA.

Because the foundation of good canoeing is good water, one of the primary concerns of the ACA is conservation and preservation of canoeable waterways and the natural environment. The Association actively

formation on an advisory service type basis. Educational and training services with emphasis on sharpening canoeing skills and increasing water safety and enjoyment are also available from the Association or from cooperative programs with the American National Red Cross, Boy Scouts, Girl Scouts, YMCA, YWCA and other national and local groups. The ACA organizes competitive canoeing such as Flatwater Paddling; Slalom and Wildwater Racing; Long Distance Racing; Canoe Poling; Sailing and Rafting. Racing rule books are provided by the Association.

### Canoe Magazine

One of the real bonuses of belonging to the ACA is the fine magazine they publish six times a year. After reviewing several issues of *Canoe*, complete with

95

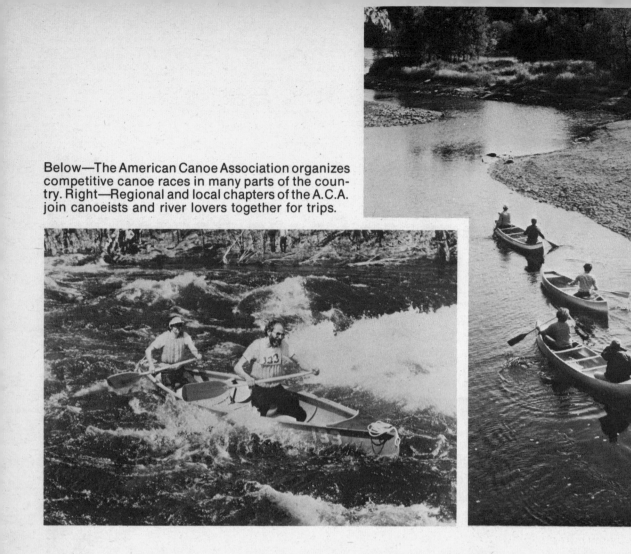

Below—The American Canoe Association organizes competitive canoe races in many parts of the country. Right—Regional and local chapters of the A.C.A. join canoeists and river lovers together for trips.

four-color covers and inside features, I found them hard to put down. Photos were good, story topics and writing were better. The novice paddler, as well as the veteran, can enjoy the magazine. The editors balance how-to's, equipment evaluation, and true canoe and kayak adventure stories. Written and edited in a professional manner, the magazine definitely incites the canoeing heart to pump faster.

An ACA membership is based on the calendar year. And all those who join after September 15th are accredited for the following year. All classes of membership—Sustaining ($14), Governing Member ($10), and Junior, those who have not reached their 18th birthday ($6)—entitle persons to participate in all local, divisional and national activities as well as to receive subscriptions to all official publications. The ACA is divided into 13 geographic divisions, and activities in the individual, self-governing divisions are determined by the interests of the members and the available canoeing waters.

Membership applications can be obtained by writing: American Canoe Association National Office, 4260 East Evans Avenue, Denver, Colorado 80222 or by telephone: (303) 758-8257.

In addition to the ACA, the American Whitewater Affiliation (AWA) is a volunteer organization of paddlers and clubs interested in white water sport. The AWA publishes the bi-monthly *American Whitewater Journal*, which offers entertaining float features along with up-to-date information on techniques, equipment, safety, conservation, racing and river access develop-

ments as well as a complete listing of affiliated clubs and how to contact them.

The AWA publishes an excellent pocket *Safety Code* for river boating in canoe, kayak or raft. Individual membership is $5 per year and club affiliation is $10 per year. For applications write: American Whitewater Affiliation, P.O. Box 1584, San Bruno, CA 94066.